THE GENESIS FILES

Edited by Carl Wieland

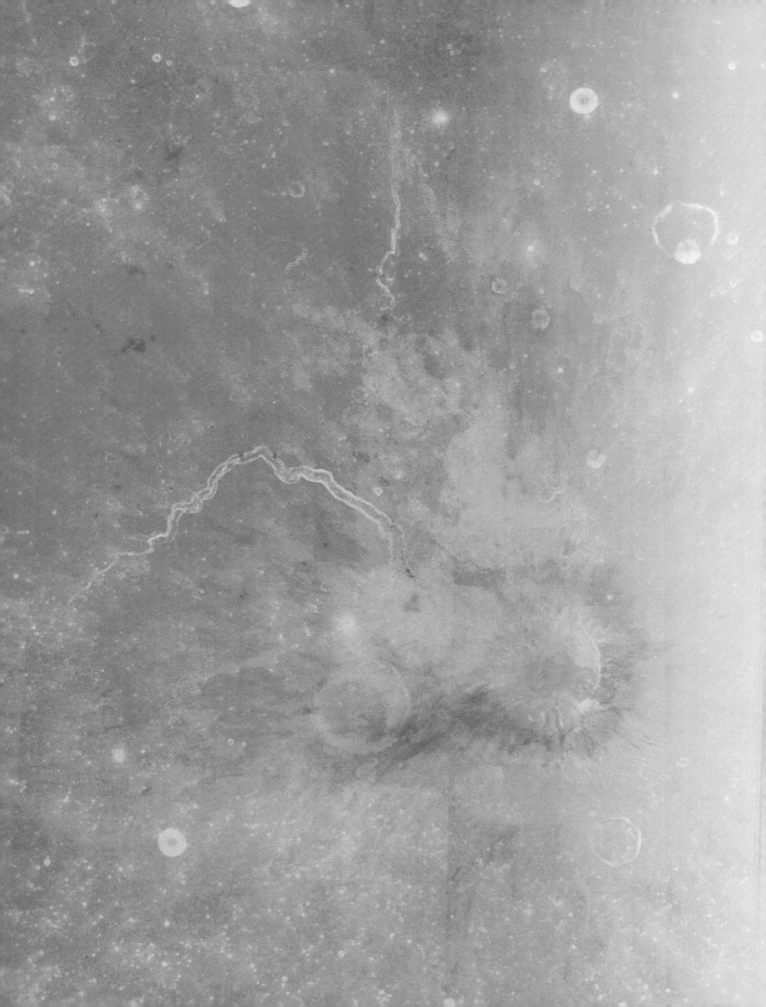

THE
GENESIS FILES

Edited by Carl Wieland

Master Books

Printed in the United States of America

Cover by Janell Robertson, Farewell Communications
Interior design by Brent Spurlock

All articles previously published in *Creation* magazine, Brisbane, Australia

Please visit our web site for other great titles:
www.masterbooks.net

ISBN: 0-89051-409-7
Library of Congress Catalog Number: 2003116031

CONTENTS

INTRODUCTION

All real scientists believe in evolution." In today's world, it's as if we're continually absorbing information from every direction which seems to reinforce this belief. But it is overwhelmingly false — a myth. Most people are stunned to find out that there are many highly qualified, practicing, professional scientists who are convinced of the truth of origins as given to us by the Creator — in Genesis. I don't just mean some vague, fuzzy notion of "God did it," but miraculous creation in six 24-hour days; a global earth-destroying Flood; and a universe that is thousands, not billions, of years old.

The number of scientists actively involved in creation outreach is relatively small. But there are *tens of thousands* of scientists going about their everyday work and research who find absolutely no reason in science to bow to the idols of evolutionary humanism.

The chapters in *The Genesis Files* are actually 22 separate articles. Each one lets the reader meet a scientist who totally believes in the Genesis history of the world. Each is very qualified and some of them are world leaders/achievers in their field. Based on direct interviews, the articles come with colorful photography which brings home that these are real live people, not some abstract concept. They were chosen to present a wide range of disciplines, and to make powerful teaching points about this whole issue in ways easy for the layperson not only to understand, but utilize in sharing with others.

Each of these 22 articles was reproduced from *Creation* magazine (the flagship of the Answers in Genesis ministry) which now goes to many thousands of subscribers in 140 countries worldwide. The magazine's whole reason for existence involves breaking down myths — the myth that the world made itself; the myth that there is no evidence for creation or the Flood; the myth that one sees evolution happening; and so on. Above all, it was meant to break

down the myth that Genesis doesn't matter to Christianity. How can one stand on a Bible that can't get it right in the opening chapter? How can one blithely swallow the "millions of years" idea when it involves death, suffering, and disease long before any Fall of Adam? What sort of God would call the world "all very good" at a time when, in the long-age view, He would have been referring to a

graveyard of creatures which had been shedding billions of gallons of blood for hundreds of millions of agonizing years? Then there is the astonishingly inconsistent and cavalier way in which followers of Christ deal with the words of the Lord Jesus Christ where He repeatedly makes it clear (e.g., Mark 10:6) that people were present at the "beginning of creation," not right at the end of an interminably long creation process groaning in pain and cancer.

This is why, shortly after I produced the first copy of *Creation* in Australia more than 25 years ago, I knew that it was important to try to have, in each issue, an article which introduces a real, highly trained working scientist to readers. The 20 such "scientist interviews" presented in *The Genesis Files* were carefully selected from the nearly 100 which *Creation* has published each quarter.

The feedback from thousands of people worldwide over the years has made me immensely aware of the power of such colorful, professionally presented "meet-a-real-scientist-who-believes-Genesis" articles. They have enabled Christians worldwide to counter the popular myth that evolutionary, anti-biblical thinking (which I once used to have) is somehow derived from, or a necessary component of, good science. This is why I am very excited at the unique concept of *The Genesis Files*, presenting these 22 selected scientists together in this way. I am convinced that this is going to be an incredibly high-impact tool in the hands of readers, confronting head-on the most damaging myths of our day.

– Dr. Carl Wieland
*CEO, Answers in
Genesis International*

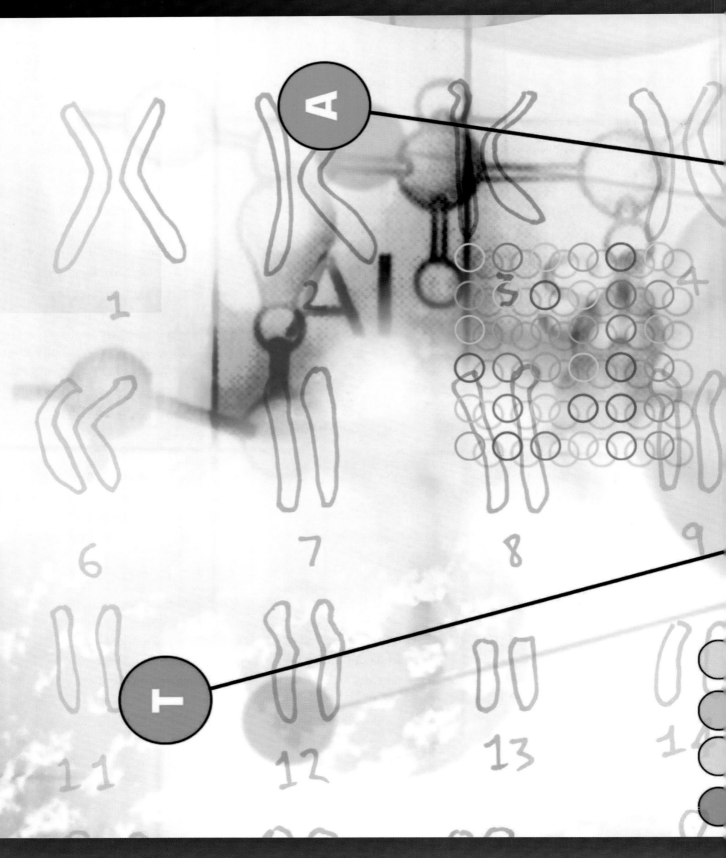

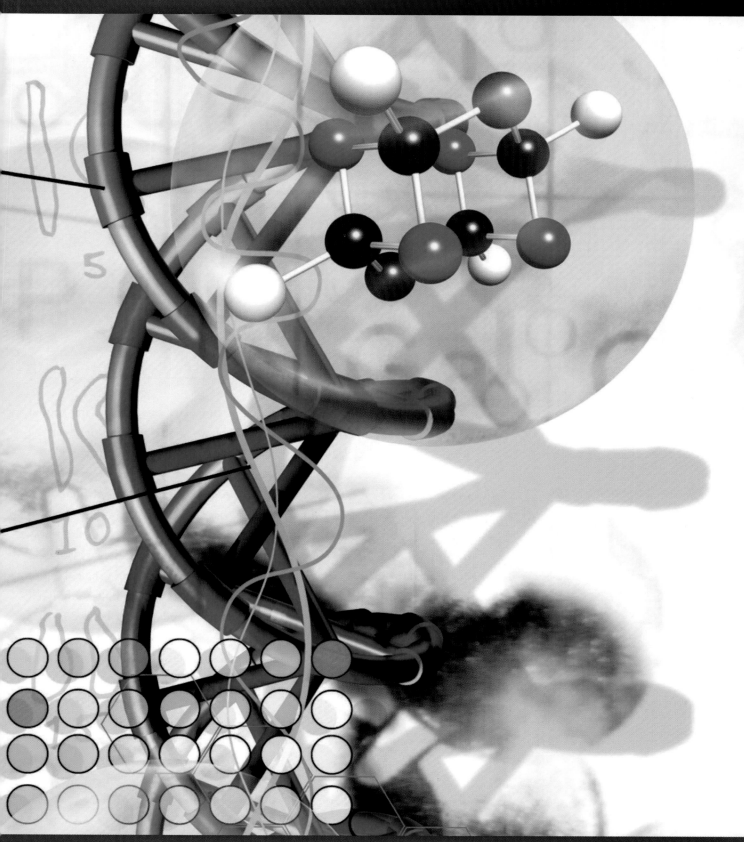

JUMPING SHIP

Dr. James Allan, M.Sc.Agric. (Stellenbosch), Ph.D. (Edinburgh), retired as senior lecturer in the Department of Genetics, University of Stellenbosch, South Africa, in 1992. He has researched the genetics of fruit flies, snails, chickens, dairy cattle, and fish, and taught students quantitative and population genetics, particularly in its application to the breeding of animals. He spoke with Dr. Don Batten and Dr. Carl Wieland.

A geneticist tells of his "double conversion"

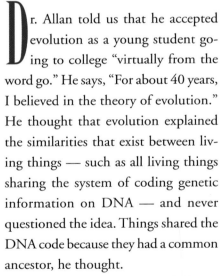

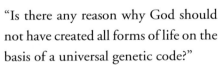

Dr. Allan told us that he accepted evolution as a young student going to college "virtually from the word go." He says, "For about 40 years, I believed in the theory of evolution." He thought that evolution explained the similarities that exist between living things — such as all living things sharing the system of coding genetic information on DNA — and never questioned the idea. Things shared the DNA code because they had a common ancestor, he thought.

Jim started to go to a different church and heard the gospel of Jesus Christ for the first time. He says, "I saw my weaknesses, my sin, my faults. I was converted and I began to read Scripture really meaningfully for the first time."

However, he carried on believing in evolution, until one day his wife said,

"Is there any reason why God should not have created all forms of life on the basis of a universal genetic code?"

Jim shared his response: "My immediate reaction was one of annoyance. What is she going on about? — absolute nonsense! What does she know about such things? And then I got up in a state of irritation and I stalked out of the house. As I walked, I found myself thinking, and I really believe at that stage God spoke to me. He humbled me. I suddenly found myself thinking, *You know, maybe she does have a point. Maybe God* did *create all forms of life on the basis of a universal genetic code.* I mean, why should we expect God to do otherwise?

"This whole argument of DNA — the universality of DNA — is a

Dr. James Allan

major plank of the common ancestry argument. I became aware that the Word of God was more important than my concept of science. And I truly can say that I became aware that I'd been worshiping and serving created things rather than the Creator, as Paul said (Romans 1:25)."

Jim says he had a "double conversion" — his spiritual conversion and his conversion from evolution to accepting creation. He says that this brought about a "radical change" in the way he regarded God. He says that previously, he had a god of his own making, one he kept "in a box," not the God of the Bible. But now, the beauty, perfection, and the wonder of the Scriptures just "jump out" at him.

We asked him how he now viewed the supposed evidence for evolution. He said, "I began to look more critically at the assumptions underlying some of those things that seemed so logical. For example, I came to see that resemblances between taxonomic families, orders, classes, etc. are due to the work of a creator, not common ancestry." Jim Allan says that previously, when people brought up creationist interpretations of the evidence he would say, "Why bring that nonsense to me? It's not science."

But in the last decade or so, as he has considered a number of these, he has found that they are perfectly reasonable and intellectually acceptable. He now finds it sad that anyone should insist

on evolutionary interpretations, which are "unproven and unprovable." "Science," he says, "becomes much more meaningful and satisfying in the light of Scripture, rather than in rejecting it. And I certainly believe it is only as we consider, together with legitimate science, the truth learned from Scripture, that we can ever really understand and appreciate the physical universe in which we live."

What about the six days of creation? Jim says, "Jesus refers in various ways to the earliest part of Scripture and says that no part of the Scripture can be broken [John 10:35]. A lot of people I have spoken to have said, 'Well, you know, I believe in Jesus Christ, but I don't believe — no, no, no — it doesn't have to be in six days.' But God did

The coyote (above) and the wolf (below), descended from the same created kind, are interfertile. Dr. Allan explains that this differs from evolution.

For since the creation of the world God's invisible qualities — his eternal power and divine nature — have been clearly seen, being understood from what has been made, so that men are without excuse.
— Romans 1:20

not say it took Him six billion years to do this and then He rested for a billion years. It says six days. And I believe six days. It has brought me a vastly greater awareness of the reality of God. If you think in terms of millions of years to now, you automatically think of millions of years in the future. And God, Scripture, Jesus Christ, and saving grace all become something rather wishy-washy and lost in the midst of this vastness.

"But if one accepts six creation days and the genealogies of Scripture, so the time overall is a question of about six thousand years — this is something the human mind can comprehend more clearly, and it brings, for me, the whole reality of God so much closer."

Dr. Allan says that when he was a "Christian evolutionist," he had not thought of the fact that believing that the fossils formed millions of years before man meant that there was death and bloodshed before sin. However, he was now acutely aware of the problem. He is now crystal clear about it; God created in perfection, and there was no death in the world until Adam sinned.

Asked how he coped as a creationist university lecturer, he said he used to give two lectures on evolution. One was what the theory said, and the other why he didn't believe it.

We raised the issue of new species forming by natural selection, to which he replied, "It doesn't matter if one population breaks into several subgroups, even to the extent of not reproducing with each other anymore. In fact, you would expect that to happen after the Flood, so coyotes, wolves, dingoes, and so on might have had a common ancestor, but the key is that there's no new information — that natural processes don't create any new DNA information. I've observed 40 generations of selection of fruit flies. I've seen lots of defective flies because of mutations, but I've never seen new, additional genetic information appear which would give hope to evolutionists. The belief in amoeba-to-man evolution needs a huge amount of new genetic information."

Having retired from secular education, Dr. Allan now lectures in churches, schools, and universities on the reality of biblical creation.

Acclaimed inventor backs creation ministry

Raymond V. Damadian
Patent No. 3,789,832
apparatus and method
for detecting cancer in tissue

Raymond V. Damadian, born on March 16, 1936, in Forest Hills, New York, is the inventor of the magnetic resonance imaging (MRI) machine which is in use in medical institutions around the world. MRI produces images of the body that are far more detailed than x-rays which it obtains from the human body through the use of static and dynamic magnetic fields.

Dr. Raymond V. Damadian would probably be too humble to accept the title "super-scientist" — but the many people whose lives have been saved by the MRI (magnetic resonance imaging) scanning technology he developed might think otherwise.

Hailed as one of the greatest diagnostic breakthroughs ever, this technique, using advanced principles of physics and computing, lets doctors visualize many organs and their diseased parts without the risks of exploratory surgery or the radiation associated with traditional scanning methods.

Hall of fame

Dr. Damadian's invention has earned him several top awards, including the United States National Medal of Technology, the Lincoln-Edison Medal, and induction into the National Inventors Hall of Fame alongside Thomas Edison, Alexander Graham Bell, and the Wright brothers.

A Bible-believing Christian, this great inventor is convinced of the scientific truth of Genesis creation and its foundational importance to church and society.

Despite his fame, however, life has had its difficulties for this revolutionizer of medicine.

SPIRITUAL SICKNESS!

First, there were the years of hard work against much opposition and many doubters. His interest in the idea of MRI began when he was a young professor engaged in active scientific research at the State University of New York. Skeptics sarcastically informed him that to use the then-young technique of nuclear magnetic resonance in a medical imaging machine would mean rotating the patient at 10,000 revolutions per minute!

He said that "theoretical physicists claimed to have done calculations demonstrating that my idea was beyond what the theory of physics would allow." This worried and confounded would-be financial backers, but Dr. Damadian took it as a challenge for himself as an "experimentalist" to "do something the theorists say can't be done."

Finally, he was granted a U.S. patent for a functioning MRI machine. Today, MRI is a world-famous, multibillion-dollar technology with more than 4,000 of these complex machines installed around the world. Dr. Damadian told *Creation* magazine of how his company, formed to exploit the legal patent with great potential benefits to many Americans, experienced something extraordinary. Several huge overseas

and multi-national firms began manufacturing MRI scanners in spite of his patent. Dr. Damadian's small company was forced to go to court — a jury trial in 1982 found the patent to be valid and infringed upon. He had won!

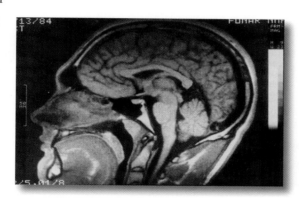

(Above) Magnetic Resonance Imaging shows detail never shown before by diagnostic imaging.

(Opposite) The history-making prototype of Dr. Damadian's MRI scanner. The first MR image of a human skull was made with this scanner on July 3, 1977. The prototype is now on permanent display at the Smithsonian Institution's Hall of Medical Sciences.

The happiness, however, was short-lived. For some reason, the judge, six weeks after the trial, "voided the jury's verdict and substituted his own." Dr. Damadian had lost. He says that after his company had spent $2.2 million in legal fees he learned the difficulties of a "little fellow" inventing a BIG product. Undaunted, his small company

nevertheless carved a niche in the marketplace. However, the really huge rewards are going overseas, to companies which were not involved in the invention at all.

Symptom of sickness

Dr. Damadian points out that this apparent injustice (shared by the inventors of such things as the laser, tetracycline, the Early Stall Warning device, and many more) was even more economically damaging to the United States than to himself. In reality, he says, it is just "a symptom of a more widespread disease afflicting our society." He believes that America is ailing spiritually. Influenced more and more by an evolution-based humanistic education system, America is adrift of its spiritual moorings.

Can such a society, with its relative ethics and increasing abandonment of God's absolute standards revealed in the Bible, "continue to discern the just from the unjust?" he asks. Will not such a society more and more forfeit the blessings which its forefathers wrought through obedience to God's law?

He quotes Russian writer Alexander Solzhenitsyn as saying, "The strength or weakness of a society depends more on the level

Dr. Raymond Damadian receives the nation's highest honor in technology, the National Medal of Technology, from President Ronald Reagan. (Inset) The National Medal of Technology.

of its spiritual life than on its level of industrialization." Without the general adherence of a society to God's laws, the most perfect governmental system cannot prevent eventual collapse. "Freedom" will deteriorate to be "freedom to be unscrupulous," because, says Solzhenitsyn, there is no law which can anticipate or prevent this.

Highest purpose

Dr. Damadian says emphatically that his greatest scientific discovery was to find that "the highest purpose a man can find for his life is to serve the will of God." He recently attended a major seminar at which he heard creation speaker Ken Ham calling for Americans to return to trust in the whole Word of God, "beginning with Moses and the prophets." He

says that he is tremendously encouraged by the creation science ministry and blessed by it, calling it "a courageous exposition of the truth" and a vitally important message for America today.

He believes that rejection of God's account of creation as the foundation for our society is basic to the spiritual, social, and economic sickness of our times. We are replaying "the seven steps of human regression and social disintegration" which the apostle Paul described as being subsequent to the rejection of the true God as Creator.

If Genesis cannot be accepted *unqualified*, what else in Scripture can be taken as the *unqualified* Word of God? Acceptance of the *unqualified* Word of God "has been the foundation for Western civilization since the printing of the Gutenberg Bible in the 15th century," he says. This has resulted in 200 years of blessing for Western civilization, including a level of individual freedom "unprecedented in human history."

Dr. Damadian says, "If America is to be rescued, she must be rescued from the pulpit — it is too late for the White House." He says that Americans need to realize that any country "runs off its spiritual batteries, not off its bank accounts, and when those batteries are drained, its bank accounts will be empty."

The 1989 National Inventors Hall of Fame inductees. Dr. Damadian is second on the left.

Following Up — *A Not-so-Nobel Drama*

After the above article was published in *Creation* magazine in 1994, two significant things took place:

1) In 1997, the U.S. Supreme Court overruled in Dr. Damadian's favor in the matter of his rights to the patent.

2) In 2003, the Nobel Prize for Medicine went to this breakthrough field of diagnostic MRI scanning. It was shared by two scientists. But, to the stunned disbelief of virtually all who worked in that field, this did not include Raymond Damadian, even though the terms allow for up to three people to share the award.

The dean of the State University of New York College of Medicine on Long Island, the institution where Damadian's pioneering work was done, said, ". . . we are so disappointed, and even angry . . . all of MRI rests on the fundamental work that Dr. Damadian has done here."

There is no doubt that the two scientists who were honored, Dr. Paul Lauterbur and Sir Peter Mansfield, did contribute to the field. Lauterbur developed techniques for producing images from scans, and Mansfield refined the techniques to make them more practical. But there is absolutely no question that the pioneering breakthroughs were Damadian's. He was the first to point out, in a landmark 1971 paper in *Science* (based on experiments involving lab rats), that MRI could be used to distinguish between healthy and cancerous tissue. Lauterbur's own notes indicate that he was inspired by Damadian's work.

In the definitive 840-page book *The Pioneers of NMR in Magnetic Resonance in Medicine: The Story of MRI,* chapter 8 is given over to Dr. Damadian. The chapter title is: "Raymond V. Damadian: Originator of the Concept of Whole-body NMR Scanning (MRI) and Discoverer of the NMR Tissue Relaxation Differences That Made It Possible." And in 2001, the Lemelson-MIT program bestowed its lifetime achievement award on Dr. Damadian as "the man who invented the MRI scanner."

All of which makes the exclusion of Dr. Damadian as the third co-recipient of the Nobel so pointed that even some of the secular media have talked of the likely link between Dr. Damadian's exclusion and his creationism.

This is important, because anti-creationists often try to pretend that there is no prejudice against biblical creation in "the world of science." But creationists have long known that things are not like that in the real world. This is why they publish their own peer-reviewed journals; any paper which does not bow to materialistic axioms on origins has virtually no chance of getting published in a secular journal.

The *New York Times* raised the issue in a recent report on Damadian's having won a Franklin Institute award "for taking amazing technology that he has legitimate claim for inventing and taking that technology to market successfully." Even *Scientific American* said that there is "no question that Damadian played a key role in the development of MRI

machines routinely used in hospitals today. The Nobel committee's decision in this case, however, seemed to be an intentional slap in Damadian's face."

Michael Ruse is an atheist Canadian philosophy professor who has fought creationism in high profile U.S. court cases. Even he has written of his own deep concern. Choosing words carefully, he writes of the "likely hypothesis" that Damadian was rejected because of his open belief in Genesis creation. Ruse says that in the eyes of the Nobel committee, "It is bad enough that such people exist, let alone give them added status and a pedestal from which to preach."

But although Ruse says he cannot help a "certain sympathy" for this view, his sense of fair play leads him to write, "I cringe at the thought that Raymond Damadian was refused his just honor because of his religious beliefs." By those standards, he points out, the Nobel committee (whose deliberations remain sealed for 50 years) would also have had to reject the late Sir Isaac Newton — the greatest scientist who ever lived and a firm Bible–believing creationist.

References and notes

James Mattson and Merrill Simon, *The Pioneers of NMR in Magnetic Resonance in Medicine: The Story of MRI* (Jericho, NY: Bar-Ilan University Press, 1996).

K. Chang, "Denied Nobel for MRI, He Wins Another Prize, *New York Times*, March 23, 2004.

M. Ruse, "The Nobel Prize in Medicine — Was There a Religious Factor in This Year's (Non) Selection?" *Metanexus Online Journal*, March 16, 2004.

Chang-Sha Fang B.Sc. (Hons.), M.Sc., is a scientist who is also a dedicated supporter of creation ministry, but it wasn't always that way. He was born in a small Malaysian village called Kampong Koh. His great-grandfather (a Methodist pastor) pioneered this village by moving all of his parishioners and his own family from mainland China as settlers. Even Chang-Sha's own name was given to him by his grandfather to commemorate the Battle of Chang-Sha, a famous battle of the Sino-Japanese war (just prior to World War II) in which the Chinese halted the Japanese advance.[1]

Despite having this strong Christian heritage (his own father was also a pastor), Chang-Sha was to face his own battle in years to come.

Believing God and His Word was not an issue when growing up in the Fang household. He explains, "Bible stories and verses were read all the time and the entirety of God's Word was believed. No one ever challenged the validity of the Bible and we had never concerned ourselves with the theory of evolution, as it wasn't emphasized in school science classes back then."

Chang-Sha eventually encountered the theory of evolution "full on" when at 19 years of age he left for Australia to study zoology and biology at Perth's University of Western Australia (UWA). He remembers that when the subject of creation was raised, it was always regarded as religion. But evolution was taught as fact.

"Being from an Asian background where we hold teachers in great respect, I felt too intimidated to challenge their authority," he says. "Because they were teachers, you believed they must be right. Remarkably, no one else ever questioned what was being taught, either."

Without the support of his family and Christian fellowship, and with the constant indoctrination of evolution being taught as fact by his lecturers, Chang-Sha says, "I graduated out of college with barely any faith left, wondering — how could my family have been wrong for all of these years?

The BATTLE of CHANG-SHA

Gary Bates talks to plant scientist Chang-Sha Fang

"I had an inquiring mind, and, like a 'doubting Thomas' (John 20: 24–29), I required evidence to counter my disbelief."

Perhaps they were just naïve and didn't know the truth? The final straw came when he asked a research colleague, a Christian, about Noah's flood. He answered that he didn't know but just believed by faith. "He didn't have any evidence or any answers for me and even suggested that Adam and Eve were just stories."

Chang-Sha can understand that for some, their parents' foundation may be enough. But he says, "I had an inquiring mind, and, like a 'doubting Thomas' (John 20: 24–29), I required evidence to counter my disbelief."

After Chang-Sha married, his wife, Barbara, became a Christian. Having no difficulties with the creation account in Genesis, she would often show him snippets of information and creationist articles that she came across.

The turning point came during a visit by his mother from Singapore, when one night after dinner Chang-Sha told her that he was not attending church anymore. A large debate ensued. "I told her that the Bible was a collection of stories and that Jesus was just a good teacher

and philosopher," he says. "I knew my mother's heart must have been stabbed to the core."

His godly mother, devastated by her son's departure from faith, arranged for groups of friends and family to pray around the clock for her son's salvation.

He says, "God was so merciful and gracious, because he met me where I was at! My research was not going well at the time and I was also frustrated due to the internal conflict I was going through. Unable to counter me with scientific arguments, my wife and mother gave me a book of sermons to read.

After reading how Jesus healed the woman with the issue of blood (Matthew 9:20–22), God spoke to me through one of the sermons and said, clearly, 'I am the Creator and I can deliver you from your frustration. Just reach out to me.' I was convicted of my need of God and my sin of denying Him. I broke down and cried like a child."

God is so good. Shortly after, Ken Ham and Dr. Gary Parker visited Perth and Chang-Sha attended the meetings, where they spoke about the complexity in created things — design and the relevance of creation to the gospel of Christ. Chang-Sha says, "After listening to them, I realized that I had been totally deceived by the false science of evolution, which had caused me to become spiritually blind.

"I bought so many books and devoured them one after the other. At the same time God provided me with a good teacher in the Scriptures. Now I was so excited at all of this new information from the Bible and *Answers in Genesis*, but at the same time I also felt

angry, because for so many years I had been brainwashed to believe the lie of evolution and deny my Creator and Savior."

As a scientist trained in plant pathology, he comments that he can now see in his work the awe-inspiring beauty and design of the Creator, but laments that during his many years spent researching and studying, he was blind to the Maker's handprint. "I feel I was deprived at not having been able to do my work wearing biblical glasses," he says.

He is currently employed as the collections manager at the Western Australian Herbarium of the Department of Conservation and Land Management in Perth. The Herbarium collects and catalogues all plants and plant matter found in Western Australia. Its database of over 550,000 plant specimens (one of only two complete plant databases in Australia) acts as a complete resource for taxonomic and conservation research for over 12,500 species of Western Australian plants.

Chang-Sha often uses the incredible design features of plants in his witnessing. However, he also explains how the selective breeding of some plant species to enhance particular characteristics of interest (such as taste or color) has resulted in a *loss* of genetic information in the selected variety. He points out that this sort of "downhill" trend is an inevitable consequence of selection, artificial or natural. In a population with lots of variety, those individuals which do not get to pass on their genes have some characteristics which are then lost to that population. As a result, one can get very "specialized" organisms, such as the highly bred dog varieties, but they carry only a fraction of the total information that was in the original population.

Although selection can cause great changes (always within a created "kind"), even to the extent of new species[2] (speciation), it can easily be shown, he says, that this sort of change is not related to the sort of process that would have been necessary to turn a microbe into a man over millions of years.

Chang-Sha is aware that evolution, as commonly understood ("goo-to-you"), must supposedly have been capable of generating lots of new genetic information that was nowhere in the world previously. He also knows from his own field of science that selection can only "choose" from the genetic information that is already there in that population. This is so, whether selection is done artificially, through selective breeding, or occurs in nature by differential survival/reproduction ("survival of the fittest"). It cannot create any new information. Mutations, genetic copying mistakes, are supposed to do so, but so far no one has seen even one of the many information-adding mutations that should be present. Even those few which give a survival benefit turn out to be losses of information.[3]

The case of the domestication of the lupin plant, *Lupinus angustifolius*, is used by Chang-Sha to illustrate how selection loses information. The full domestication of this species, combining the sweetness gene with the non-shattering pod, was one of the success stories of plant breeders in Western Australia. As this species was especially adapted to sandy soils, sweet cultivars of lupin soon

became a very popular alternative grain crop for farmers. Unfortunately, the new cultivars were found to be susceptible to anthracnose[4] disease. In selecting attributes for sweetness, non-shattering of pods, and other yield attributes, the resistance for anthracnose disease was lost.

Similarly, blackleg[5] disease of oilseed rape (canola) devastated the industry in Australia in the early 1970s. To obtain the genes for resistance to this disease, which genes had been lost in the process of selecting for other attributes, plant breeders in Australia had to return to the "original population" from which the resistance had been lost — oilseed rape stocks in Europe.

By "back-crossing" with these European plants, genes conferring resistance to blackleg were transferred to Australian cultivars. "It seems obvious," says Chang-Sha, "that selection gets rid of information; it doesn't create any, and so is the opposite of what is supposed to have happened in microbe-to-man evolution. But many people think that once you have an example of something adapting by selection, you have an example of evolution. So, it almost can't be pointed out often enough."

Chang-Sha is currently the leader of AiG's Perth-based West Australian Support Group. He says, "It's my own past experiences that continue to motivate my involvement in this way. Because it's not good enough when Christians or their pas-

> *"It seems obvious that selection gets rid of information; it doesn't create any, and so is the opposite of what is supposed to have happened in microbe-to-man evolution."*

tors say they don't know how it happened or that this is a technical issue. Today, we can provide answers and ensure that the message gets out there. People need never be brainwashed by the lie of evolution. There's no excuse!"

References and notes

1. This 1939 battle is not to be confused with the 1942 battle, also at Chang Sha (Mao Zedong's home town), hailed as the first major allied victory of WWII.

2. The usual definition of species is meant, namely reproductive isolation.

3. Wieland, C., Beetle bloopers, <www.answersingenesis.org/beetle>, *Creation* 19(3):30, 1997.

4. Anthracnose disease is caused by a fungus. Symptoms include bending of stems, lesions, and death of leaves and stems above these lesions.

5. Blackleg disease is caused by a fungus that affects the roots, causing stunted growth and possible death of the plant.

Geniuses for Genesis

Mark Looy interviews William Ho and Esther Su

This is an amazing family: four siblings who all entered college by the age of 14 or younger (one at the age of 10!). In the eyes of the secular world, what makes them even more amazing is that these exceptionally gifted children (now adults) believe in the Bible from the very first verse, including the historic and scientific reliability of the Book of Genesis.

The Ho children — Samuel, Adina, Susanna, and Sean — are the four remarkable children of Dr. William Ho (M.D.)[1] and his wife, Dr. Esther Su (Ph.D., biochemistry).[2] Fleeing the communist revolution in China of the late 1940s, Dr. Ho settled in Hong Kong, where he received his medical qualification, and then emigrated to the United States in 1964.

His fiancée, Esther Su, had already moved to the United States from Hong Kong and was finishing her Ph.D. in biochemistry at the University of Michigan. (They had grown up together in Hong Kong.) Their life stories and Christian testimonies (to follow later) are fascinating in and of themselves, but when interviewed, these parents concentrated on their four exceptional children and how the Lord was equipping and using them for ministry.

Son Samuel — entered the University of Washington (Seattle) at age 10! He completed his mathematics degree at 13, and earned a Ph.D. in computer science at the age of 22. He is currently working in computer research in Massachusetts.

Daughter Adina — enrolled in the University of Washington at age 14 and received two bachelor's degrees by the age of 19 (in chemistry and music). She then obtained graduate degrees in genetics and psychology (four different degrees in all), and is currently a school psychologist in Massachusetts.

Daughter Susanna — entered the University of Washington at age 14, and earned two bachelor's degrees by the age of 18 (in chemistry and biochemistry). By age 26, she had earned an M.D. *and* a Ph.D. (in molecular genetics) from Harvard Medical School.

Son Sean — enrolled in the University of Washington at age 13, and by the age of 20, had earned both a B.S. and M.S. in mathematics. He is currently finishing his Ph.D. in computer science at the University of North Carolina.

In an interview conducted with Dr. Su in North Carolina (with son Sean at her side), she revealed that what makes her most happy about her four children is not their incredible scholastic accomplishments, but that they are believers in Jesus Christ — and that they actively share their faith in one-on-one evangelism and through public lectures. Each one gives illustrated presentations on Bible/science topics to a wide range of audiences.

The children's father, Dr. Ho, gives credit to his wife in raising their four "unusual children," as he termed them. "In my family, God has given me a loving and saintly wife who has all but sacrificed her career in biochemistry to care for our children, who now serve actively at church."

Now that Dr. Ho has given up his medical practice, he devotes most of his time to speaking on a wide range of issues, including creation versus evolution (which is one of the most-requested topics he receives).

At dinner, Sean (at age 23, the youngest sibling) made a mock apology for being the slacker in the family because he had not yet finished his Ph.D.! He does not know where the Lord will eventually use him and his ability in computer science, but he informed me that he will definitely use his future job as a platform for sharing his faith.

Susanna told me that she "came to know Christ at age three, under the guidance of my parents." As a 26-year-old biochemist, her years of study on the complexity of living things have shown

(Above) Sean and his mother on a field trip to Mount St. Helens in Washington.

(Opposite) The Ho family enjoying an evening (from left: son-in-law Ivan, Susanna, William, Esther, Samuel, Adina, and Sean).

Drs. William Ho and Esther Su

her that "only He, the Creator, could have called life into being. Having realized firsthand the amount of research it takes to even begin to understand one small function of a single-celled organism," she continued. "I appreciate the designing wisdom of the One who created all of life."

Adina, now 30, shared with us that she "grew up in an environment saturated with Scripture. The Bible was read to us before we were out of the womb!" She received the Lord at age four, and from that point she was encouraged by her parents to use her "God-given reason to explore the objective reasons for accepting the Bible as literal and scientific truth."

At age nine, Adina was already taking university classes, but her parents decided not to enroll her full-time when they discovered that she would be saturated in strong anti-Christian, evolution-based teaching, and so they placed her instead in a solid Christian high school.

In her profession as a school psychologist, Adina sees the consequences of the fall of mankind on a daily basis. "I witness the truth of Genesis displayed in the brokenness of sin-defiled humanity. Spiritual, physical, and emotional decay in children are striking reminders of the disobedience of our first parents, and the decay that entered all people through them."

Samuel, the eldest, lives near his sister Adina, and is a senior engineer for a major computer firm located in the Boston area (where he designs computer chips).

As an occasional lecturer on such topics as cosmology and physics from a Genesis perspective, Samuel uses many of his parents' overhead illustrations to

Dr. William Ho during a visit to Hawaii.

help teach audiences that the Bible and real science are not in conflict. As he grew up, his parents taught him not to fear the pursuit of knowledge, and so even as he examined the thorny question of the age of the earth, he saw from both Scripture and science that the world is young. He commented, "Biblically, it makes sense, and the only reason evolutionists want an old earth is to have enough time for evolution to occur."

Samuel believes that the creation-versus-evolution issue is a vital one, because "where we come from is the foundation of everything we believe." Further, "When we have the right starting point — Genesis — science makes sense. Too many scientists build on a wrong foundation — evolution."

Nature versus nurture?

Dr. Su politely sidestepped the question as to whether or not her children's remarkable intellect has something to do with genetics, other than to say that "all children are gifted, and those gifts are given to them by their Creator. Parents are responsible for nurturing and developing what their children have already been given."

The familiar "nature versus nurture" riddle, she says, "is for others to figure out. What you teach children, however, is far more important than their capacity to learn. You see, if you teach a smart kid that he evolved from monkeys, he will perhaps act like one. But if he's convinced that he's created in God's image, he will be more inclined to know that there is right and wrong, spiritual laws designed by the Creator. When we follow them (the 'manufacturer's instructions'), our lives will go well."

The parents

The four Ho children are so well grounded, both academically and biblically, because of the training they received from their godly and high-achieving parents. While a college student, however, Dr. Su had to struggle over the creation-versus-evolution issue and the authority of the Bible. She decided to systematically tackle two areas: "I therefore set up for myself basic questions to answer in order to prove scientifically whether or not the earth and universe were created, and then to determine if the Bible was true.

"I discovered that science was very limited because scientists can only study the present. Science requires observation, but you can't observe the past. So, the question of whether or not the universe was created is a historical question, not a scientific one. The question should be whether or not the evidence we observe today supports creation or evolution."

Dr. Su conducted an intensive study into three areas. First, she looked at paleontology. "If evolution is true," she posited, "then there must be all kinds of 'in-between' forms of creatures."

She discovered that the fossil record, as well as observations of living things, supports the creation account, that all things reproduce "after their kind" (ten times in Genesis). "When I was able to distinguish between the facts of science and the opinions of some scientists, the truth was obvious," she added.

Second, she looked at biochemistry, her field of expertise, and saw tremendous complexity in living things — telltale signs of a Master Designer. "The design of life is something that cannot be explained without a Creator. Even a so-called 'simple' cell is so very complicated."

A family celebration of Susanna's graduation from Harvard University.

Dr. Su then carefully studied biblical prophecy, and discovered that what the Old Testament foretold about the coming of Christ all came true. "There were just so many prophecies — and so much detail — about the coming Messiah." So, during graduate school, and after much study of the Bible, she says, "I gave myself to God the Creator."

Drs. Ho and Su expressed their gratitude for organizations such as *Answers in Genesis* that uphold the authority of the Bible from the very first verse. Their study of both science and Scripture also leads them to agree with AiG that the earth is young, not millions of years old — and that the very gospel message itself is tied to that issue.

She said, "For this, the words of Scripture and the opinions of theologians need to be distinguished. Death of creatures before Adam and Eve's sin could never have happened. If it did, death is not the result of sin. 'Sin' means missing the mark, or being not ideal. A non-ideal ball that does not bounce back to its original height will 'die' — not bounce forever. But death *is* the result of sin (Romans 5:12), so when Jesus Christ died in our stead and rose

again, He conquered death and took care of the sin problem. When we, who have inherited Adam's non-ideal life, trust in Christ, He gives us His own life which is ideal, and therefore eternal."

Dr. Ho reported that this vital doctrine of "no death before Adam's Fall" is a wonderfully effective evangelistic tool. He declared that through such teaching from Genesis, "people receive Christ at almost all of our meetings."

Indeed, that's the aim of the AiG ministry worldwide — to use "creation evangelism" to break down the stumbling blocks that non-Christians have to being receptive to the gospel message.

It is encouraging to know that these six very gifted and highly intelligent Christians are presenting the life-changing creation/gospel message to so many people.

References and notes

1. Dr. Ho's medical qualification is M.B., B.S., the British equivalent of the American M.D.

2. For thousands of years, women in China have not changed their last names upon getting married. Once Chinese parents give their children a name, it is very unusual for them to change it.

Don Batten and Carl Wieland talk to Raymond Jones

Leuceana, the shrubby tree introduced to Australia's seasonally dry tropics to increase beef production, caused the cattle grazing it to become sick and thin. Dr. Raymond Jones, who recently retired from Australia's highly respected government scientific body, CSIRO, after 38 years of service, is best known for solving this problem.

This, combined with Dr. Jones's other achievements in improving the productivity of the tropical grazing industries, caused CSIRO chief Dr. Elizabeth Heij to describe him as "one of the top few CSIRO scientists in Australia." Among the awards he has received are the CSIRO Gold Medal For Research Excellence, and the Urrbrae Award, the latter in recognition of the practical significance of his work for the grazing industry.

Dr. Jones was officer-in-charge of the CSIRO Davies Laboratory, Townsville, and Regional Research Leader. He is a Fellow of the Australian Institute of Agricultural Science, the Australian Academy of Technological Sciences and Engineering, and the Tropical Grasslands Society of Australia. He has published about 140 research papers.

DB/CW: Dr. Jones, you apparently met a lot of skepticism from other scientists about the rumen microbe idea to detoxify *Leucaena* (see sidebar page 29).

RJ: That was disappointing to me. Scientists, too, can be very parochial. I had lots of opposition. It was an accepted "fact" that rumen bacteria were the same all over the world. Even though I had shown they were not, they said it was impossible. I had papers rejected without addressing the issues they contained.

How would you react to people who say that evolution must be right because most scientists agree with it?

Standing Firm
A leading scientist's life shows how radical ideas can lead to the greatest breakthroughs

Dr. Raymond Jones

"Believing in God gives you confidence that something will be found when you search, because behind it all is a mind greater than your own."

I don't think it's very sensible to say that. Major breakthroughs in science often occur when people don't believe what the rest believe. Science progresses as new ideas replace old ones. It's the radicals who often make the breakthroughs.

Are the microbes special to the ruminants?

Yes, a ruminant couldn't live on roughage without the bugs, because these digest the tough cellulose fiber in the plants the animals eat. And the bacteria are mostly highly anaerobic [do not like oxygen], and can only live in the rumen. The animal needs the microbes and the bugs need the animal. It's a good example of design. Evolutionists would argue it's "co-evolution," but I don't believe the incredible ruminant digestion system is the result of countless accidental mutations which just happened to parallel each other in the bacteria and the animals.

[Dr. Jones is well known, and respected, for his stand for Christ in his profession. He became a Christian at the age of 17, before he went to college ("fortunately," he says). His conversion was due to the faithful work of the town produce grocer, who ran a kids' club. Raymond led his gang to try to break up the grocer's meeting, but ended up (eventually) being converted.

Raymond believed in evolution before he was converted. Then he tried to believe that God directed evolution, but he realized that this contradicted the whole idea of evolution — that it's due to chance mutations. As he studied the Bible's teaching on redemption, he became increasingly skeptical of the evolutionary ideas being taught at the university. This caused him to look seriously at the evidence. He said, "As I looked at the evidence — trying to be a dispassionate scientist — I could not find the evidence for the multitudes of intermediate forms which should exist if evolution was true."]

Dogmatic statements are made that students must be taught evolution because without it science would fall apart. They even claim evolution has great practical value.

In my experience, I've never seen that. Many scientists might speculate in their papers about how a certain result relates to evolution. But I don't see that it's the driving force that enables breakthroughs, or that it features much in most scientists' daily work. Is having an evolutionary paradigm more enabling of research? I don't think so. In fact, believing in an almighty all-knowing God, rather than chance, behind everything could be more of a driving force for your scientific work. It gives you confidence that something will be found when you search, because behind it all is a mind greater than your own — "thinking God's thoughts after Him" [to quote Kepler].

How do you see the widespread indoctrination in evolution affecting society and people's ability to respond to the Gospel?

I think it's a major factor. It's a very powerful way of getting rid of God altogether because evolution is about chance, not purpose.

What about the widespread belief in millions of years of death and suffering before man appeared, sinned and caused the Fall?

It is very difficult, if you can accept that, to relate it to the message in the Bible that through sin, death came into the world. Christ died because Adam brought death into the world. It's difficult to see how that could fit the idea of millions of years of death and suffering before man sinned.

Do you have any advice for young budding scientists?

If they are Christians, continue to go on with the Lord and trust that He will reveal His will to you. Honor the Lord in all things. I found that the Lord honors those who honor Him [1 Samuel 2:30].

My advice to young scientists is to observe, observe, observe. This is the big thing. When we have so much that's done for us by computers, it's very easy to lose observational skills. In my research it's been observation on a wide scale that enabled me to understand the systems, and pick up leads to follow and reach solutions.

And not be blinded by the prevailing paradigms, or ways of thinking?

True. It's very easy to have paradigms that swamp you, but that are wrong and misleading.

What about the six creation days? There are many people who say, "I don't believe in evolution, but I don't know about six days."

I accept the biblical account of six ordinary days of creation. But humanly speaking, it's over this time situation, in areas outside my own field, like geology for example, that I have the greatest difficulty reconciling the data. On the biological side of evolution, I've no qualms, no difficulties whatsoever. But I don't believe it's irreconcilable.

We need to remember that paradigms, frameworks of thought which dominate a particular area of science, have been known to mislead. God is all-powerful, so He can do anything. So, yes, I believe in six days, as the Bible clearly says.

How long have you been receiving *Creation* magazine?

Many, many years. I read it from cover to cover. I am delighted with its regular, updating information, shedding new light on various aspects of the debate. I recommend it to others. I enrolled a scientific colleague and friend in South Africa to receive the magazine. When he got the first one he immediately wrote to thank me for sending it, and said how much he was enjoying it.

Thank you, Dr. Jones.

The *Leucaena* story

Leucaena, a legume, is a shrubby tree which grows well in the seasonally dry tropics. It remains nutritious during the dry season, when most other plants lose much of their feed value. However, *Leucaena* contains a toxin which caused animals which grazed it in Australia to become sick.

Dr. Jones discovered that goats in Hawaii ate *Leucaena* without problems. He suggested that perhaps the bacteria in the rumen (a special "stomach" where the food is pre-digested by microbes in animals such as cattle, sheep, and goats) were different in Hawaii. They were capable of breaking down the toxin, thus accounting for the lack of toxicity of *Leucaena* in Hawaii.

Other scientists scoffed at the idea that the microbes could be different and he could get no funding to check out his idea further. So Dr. Jones, convinced he was right, paid his own expenses* to go to Hawaii to follow up on the theory.

Subsequently, with funding, Dr. Jones took Australian goats and Australian grown leucaena to Indonesia where some goats had been discovered which could eat *Leucaena* without problems. He and his colleagues transferred some rumen fluid from the Indonesian goats to the Australian goats. Within two days the amount of toxin in the urine of the treated goats declined dramatically and they thrived. The theory was proven!

Eventually the microbes, isolated from goats in Hawaii, were shown to be new to science and named *Synergistes jonesii* in his honor. Their introduction to Australian ruminants proved to be successful . . . and the rest is history. As Dr. Jones says, "It turned ratbag animals into healthy ones." This discovery is worth millions of dollars per year to Australia, and is increasing as more *Leucaena* is planted.

* Subsequently reimbursed by CSIRO.

It's not every day one interviews a research scientist whose first name is "Atomic." When I first met Dr. Atomic Chuan Tse Leow, on a previous visit to Singapore, he told me his name was chosen because his father had been fascinated by the advances of the nuclear age. Atomic is well known as a passionate proclaimer of the gospel, and the total authority and inerrancy of God's Word, the Bible. After hearing his astonishing testimony of the powerful working of God in his life, this is little wonder.

WARNING: The following childhood experiences involve graphic, disturbing realities. We decided not to "paper over" these (just as the Bible gives explicit descriptions of man's evil to show us the good), because they make his subsequent conversion all the more marvelous.

When Atomic was a young child, his father sent his family to Malaysia so the children could study there, while he remained in Thailand to work the family plantation. It was bad enough that the children were deprived of a father except for two to three days each year; far worse was the fact that the coach their father had hired, one Mr. Choo, turned out to be a master of sadism and child abuse.

For eight long years, at that formative time in their lives, Atomic says, "I can hardly remember a single night where we were not bashed and tortured until we were bruised all over." These four little boys were constantly subjected to excruciating pain through such maneuvers as jamming their little fingers and toes in door hinges, or being forced to hold lit firecrackers to explode in their hands. Being made to squat for up to five hours, with consequently savage leg cramps, was common, as was being half-strangled by a cloth knot around the neck, tightened till their faces turned purple.

Even though his little sister was too young to commence tuition, says Atomic, "The senseless beating extended to her, too." On one occasion, Mr. Choo, enraged by the noise of her playing upstairs, kicked her repeatedly on the stomach "until her face turned pale and she started sweating profusely." Even on Sundays, Mr. Choo's day off, the children could not feel safe, as he would pay them surprise visits. On one Sunday, he caught Atomic reading a comic book. As punishment, he used his cigarette lighter to set the comic book on fire, and slowly roasted Atomic's legs over it. The litany of abuse even involved permanent physical injury.

The boys hated Mr. Choo, and talked of how they wanted to kill him. Not surprisingly, many of them, including Atomic, became "especially

ATOMIC POWER

Carl Wieland interviews Atomic Leow

Dr. Atomic Chuan Tse Leow Ph.D. (toxicology), B.Agr.Sc. (Hons.), Dip. C.S.[1] (*summa cum laude*), Dip. Ed., is head of the Biotechnology Specialist Unit at Singapore's Temasek School of Applied Science.

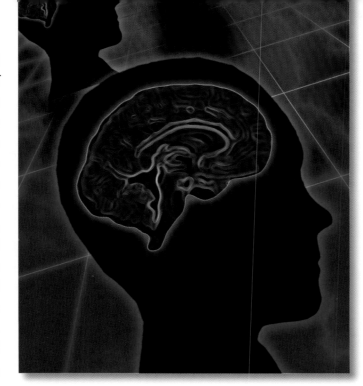

violent, aggressive, and rebellious." Two of his brothers became caught up in violent gang activities. Even Atomic's mother shattered his vulnerable heart one day by telling him she hated him, that he had "hatched from a rock" and she had just happened to pick him up from a wastewater drain. Atomic's childhood and teen years were, he says, filled with the trauma of "being unloved, beaten, and bashed, full of violent fighting and heavy indulgence in Buddhist worshiping."

Sent to Australia to study in 1968, Atomic said he vented his "anger, frustration, and unloved feelings by bashing up people who dared to confront me." Weight training and high-level martial arts skills had made him strong and fearless. Summoned by the Australian High Commission for his continual brawling, he was given a last chance to escape deportation.

On December 23, 1970, Atomic says he was so depressed that he came to the conclusion that there was no God, as He had never answered any of his prayers or reached out from heaven to save him. He recalls shouting at God to reveal himself, and if that did not happen soon, he would kill himself. The next evening he went to a huge "carols by candlelight" event in the open air. The songs, he says, were mostly about "things like reindeer noses and Santa Claus, meaningless to my troubled heart." He says he "celebrated" Christmas by beating up his unfortunate companion, and then roamed the streets, his agonized heart asking, "Who am I?"

He finally collapsed, exhausted, on his bed in the early hours, and unknowingly kicked over the electric radiator. He woke to find the radiator engulfed in flames, blue sparks dancing around its now detached live wire. After 30 minutes snuffing out the fire, he says he distinctly heard a voice commanding him to go the front foyer of the hostel, where he found a book, the Bible. The voice instructed him to flip to the first page of the book, and later to the last part. He began to read Genesis: "In the beginning, God created the heaven and the earth. Now the earth was form-less and empty, and darkness was upon the face of the deep, and the Spirit of God was hovering above the waters. . . ."

Instantly, he says, he knew that this was the very God to whom he had cried out in suicidal despair. On that Christmas Day, as he read from Revelation about God's judgment on those who would not repent, Atomic fell on his knees and accepted Jesus Christ as his personal Savior.

After this miraculous conversion, he stopped his fighting and became renowned as a caring son, husband, and father. One day, he happened to come across Mr. Choo in public. For one moment, blood rushed to his head, and all the old hurt, pain and rage returned — but only for a moment. He was able to go up to him and shake hands. He says, "This is what the mighty God can do — turn a deadened heart of stone into a heart of flesh and love. I had found forgiveness in God — He had saved a wretch like me!"

More nightmares

In 1979, Atomic had finished his Ph.D. He was on his way to a meeting at an Australian university which had asked him to apply for a position in applied science, in

Dr. Atomic Chuan Tse Leow

"There are 100 billion nerve cells . . . all integrated and functioning and connected to many others in complex circuits. Something like that cannot have come by itself, it has to be designed."

electron microscope studies. Right outside the university entrance, he heard a tremendous explosion. From 20 stories above, a 45-lb. (20-kg) drum of highly corrosive dichromic acid, used to remove rust, had fallen onto the pavement. It burst right in front of him, disgorging the powerful acid into his eyes, nose, throat, and lungs. Despite rinsing his body under a shower for hours, he suffered damage to his vision, and breathing difficulties lasting for months.

Right then, a letter came from his father in Thailand, edged in black. It said, "Son, I'm sorry, somebody has pumped two bullets into your brother and killed him."

Then his three-month-old daughter developed extremely severe allergies. There was not a patch of skin on her body which was not ulcerated, bleeding, inflamed, and oozing pus. In despair, he asked God, "Why don't you just take her, Lord?" (He now says, "I'm glad God doesn't answer stupid prayers.")

Even though he wanted to work as a forensic toxicologist, Atomic felt a strong urging to do a one-year diploma in education, to be able to teach students and change lives. But due to his daughter's severe problems, his wife had to look after her non-stop. To survive, he found night work in a Chinese restaurant, but this was barely enough to pay for his daughter's medications. They were only able to stay alive because the restaurant owner would give them a gift of one omelette each night, which they shared along with rice and the cheapest dried vegetable soup. During the day he attended his course. At night he worked in the restaurant. Then from 11 p.m. to

4 a.m. he would do his homework, then sleep for three hours.

The restaurant owner's abusive daughter had been yelling at him for months. One day, he asked her to please stop. As a result, she and her mother demanded he be sacked. He says, "Three months to go in my course, and no more omelette. What were we to do? My wife and I fell on our knees and knew we had to trust God." Amazingly, the next day, the university's dean called, exempting him from the next three months, and offering him a job as biology head in a senior college.

The university from whose premises the acid fell was fighting him in court over his residual problems from the acid incident. Twenty-seven frustrating months had passed; his wife and daughter had had to return to Singapore months previously, but he was unable to join them while the case lasted. The "opposition" hired an expensive Queen's Counsel (QC), so his lawyer recommended likewise. But the bills were horrendous, and when told that it could go on for another three years, Atomic determined that he would join his family, on faith, and abandon his court case into God's hands. Undeterred by his lawyer's warnings that pulling out would leave him open to be sued for expenses, he resigned his job and booked passage to Singapore. Packing on his last day in Melbourne, the phone rang. It was his lawyer to say that, inexplicably, the university's QC had walked into his office and offered to settle for a substantial amount.

Atomic says that as a scientist, repeatable confirmation is important to him — and over and over (there were more such profound experiences than space permits us to repeat) his life has shown the dependability of God "when there was nowhere else to turn." He says, "Each time things seemed hopeless, turning to God gave the answer, just around the corner. We should not doubt God, but cast ourselves wholeheartedly upon the Lord."

Trusting the Word

Despite these experiences, Atomic, over and over, urged me, "Please tell your readers, it is very important — don't trust in your experience, trust only in God's Word."

Knowing about his hardships, I asked him about bad things happening to Christians. He said, "God brings rain — and sunshine — to the just *and* the unjust. Why would we expect to escape bad things? They come from the curse God put on the world after Adam's sin. But in spite of the Fall, we're made in God's image, and should reflect His glory."

Having seen God at work in his life, Atomic is scornful of the notion of any mistakes in His Word about origins. In his research work, he says, "I've examined the intricacies of the brain under the electron microscope, magnified 50,000 times. The complexity and the design is staggering. We used the finest of glass pipettes to puncture the tiny gap between the nerve and muscle, the neuromuscular junction. Using this intracellular recording technique, it was truly amazing to watch. Every time a

single acetylcholine vesicle[2] arrived, a tiny electric potential (called miniature end plate potential) spiked. Surely, God's work of creation is evident even down to the microscopic level.

"There are 100 billion nerve cells (several times more glial cells[3]) all inte-

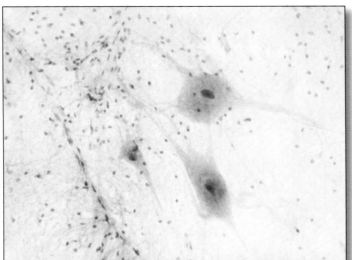
Neuron cells magnified 2000 times.

grated and functioning and connected to many others in complex circuits. Something like that cannot have come by itself, it has to be designed. I see the wonder of God everywhere in my work, it could not have come by chance. In fact, I see God everywhere in science. The stars, the complexity of DNA, the harmony of how everything all ties together."

The Bible's history of the universe is something Atomic totally believes. "The evidence for the Flood is all around us — the whole world is covered in sediments, and there are even clam shells on

top of the Himalayas." Evolution is a scientific absurdity, he maintains. "Birds are very different from reptiles. Their lungs are vastly different in terms of morphology and function. And a bird is warm-blooded, a reptile cold-blooded. The endocrine control involved in warm-bloodedness is very, very complex. Reptiles have solid bone, birds' bones are hollow. And reptiles' scales are totally different from feathers."

His passion rose. "How can life come from non-life? This is not scientific. My whole life as a research scientist confirms that life only ever comes from life. Inserting genes into another cell does not demonstrate how life could come from non-life. Evolution doesn't make sense to me."

What about the age of the earth? Atomic, a scientist, is unimpressed with claims for millions or billions of years. "I know about the fallibility of dating methods," he says. "I trust the Bible. That should be the bottom line for all of us — in everything."

References and notes

1. C.S. = Christian Studies, from the Biblical Graduate School of Theology, where he is also pursuing a Master of Divinity.

2. A tiny packet containing a chemical used to transmit nerve impulses.

3. These provide support functions for the nerve cells.

Trust in the LORD and do good; dwell in the land and enjoy safe pasture. – Psalm 37:3

Creation in the Research Lab

Carl Wieland and Don Batten
talk to Ian Macreadie

We knew Dr. Ian Macreadie (left) to be a highly respected scientist. He is at the forefront of research in a field which, in many minds, is strongly linked to evolution. So it was significant to hear him say, "I've always believed the Bible's creation account. It's beyond my comprehension that things could have just developed from nothing, and that we could have developed from 'ape' ancestors."

Dr. Macreadie said that during his education, evolution was just taught as "one of the options." However, he said, "Even though nothing much has changed since then in the way of scientific advances, now we are barraged with information presenting it as undisputed fact."

Apart from a slight wavering in his teenage years, Ian has been a committed Christian since he was about ten, after

going forward at a crusade. He first heard an *Answers in Genesis* speaker in about 1990, at a church meeting. Some time later, he accepted our

Dr. Ian Macreadie is a highly regarded Australian researcher in the fields of molecular biology and microbiology. Author of more than 60 research papers, he is a principle research scientist at the Biomolecular Research Institute of Australia's Commonwealth Scientific and Industrial Research Organisation (CSIRO),* and national secretary of the Australian Society for Biochemistry and Molecular Biology.

In 1997, he was part of a team which won CSIRO's top prize, the Chairman's Medal. In 1995, he won the Australian Society for Microbiology's top award, for outstanding contributions to research.

* In this interview, Dr. Macreadie is stating his personal opinions; he is not representing CSIRO, and claims no official CSIRO endorsement of his statements.

invitation to speak in his specialty area of science at one of our major seminars. He says that "creation is an issue that is certainly relevant to the gospel. Evolutionist thinking is one of the factors which keeps many people from even recognizing the existence of God."

We asked him about the idea that fossils, with all their implied death and bloodshed, existed millions of years before man. He said, "You really can't have death before the Fall, which means you can't have death before man." Ian sees the authority of the Bible as a foundational issue. He said, "I think every Christian needs to take that on board right from the start—we've got to accept the Bible as God's Word."

We asked Ian about the evidence for creation in his own field. He said, "Evolution would argue for things improving, whereas I see everything falling to pieces. Genes being corrupted, mutations [mistakes as DNA is copied each generation] causing an increasing community burden of inherited diseases. All things were well designed initially."

The origin of AIDS

As one of the leading AIDS researchers in the southern hemi-

sphere, Ian was in a position to comment about viruses. He said, "I actually don't believe God created viruses as separate entities, I believe they were a part of the DNA in cells. Some evolutionists put viruses down as a predecessor of cells, but that doesn't work, because they need to have the machinery of cells to reproduce. I actually see viruses as genetic garbage, having escaped from cells way back, as a result of mutation, environmental damage—part of the curse on creation [Genesis 3]. I would predict from that theory that we should find pieces of 'virus' DNA in the human genome (DNA). And that's starting to be found."

A virus, being not much more than a packet of DNA, could jump from being hosted by one species to another. So did AIDS emerge from green monkeys, as one often hears? Ian replied, "The semi-immunodeficiency virus in African green monkeys is certainly the closest thing to the AIDS virus, but we really still don't know. It's interesting—you'd think if we were so smart about man's alleged evolutionary origin, we'd be able to pick where this recently emerged virus came from."

Molecular biologists have made some awe-inspiring discoveries,

> *"Evolution would argue for things improving, whereas I see everything falling to pieces."*

but how much is really known? Ian told us that all of the 6,000 genes in the DNA of a "simple" yeast cell have now been mapped out. The function of only about half of these is known, he said, but probably less than 5 percent would be known in terms of a full understanding of the 3-D structure of the resultant protein (the molecule that is coded for by a particular gene). "Interestingly," he said, "you can have all the components together, but you can't yet create even a yeast cell, which has only a fraction of the genes of a human cell. Even with all the people working on it today, it has, so far, defied complete description—it's just amazingly complex."

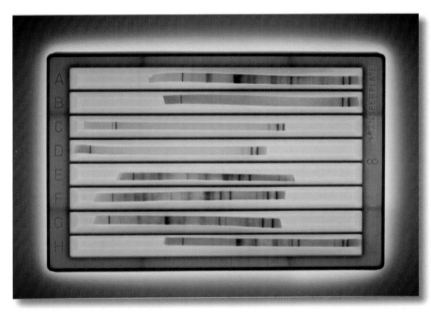

So could such complexity all be coded for in the large, but finite, amount of information in a yeast's DNA? Did he think we only needed to fine-tune our understanding about the information systems in living things, or were there likely to be some real surprises in store?

Dr. Macreadie indicated that he doubted that the current understanding would prove adequate. He said, "There have been lots of surprises in yeast; for example, some of its genes are the same as some in plants, but with a totally different function. I'm sure there will be many more surprises in human cells. In yeast, it's been discovered that the same stretch of DNA can code for different proteins, simply by shifting the 'reading frame,' starting to read the code from a different point—an amazingly ingenious way of storing extra information. And we've known for some time how a gene can be 'cut and pasted' to make several different proteins. And if that wasn't mind-boggling enough, we've recently found that a protein, made by one gene, can also be spliced and directed to two different locations in the cell."

Mutations — no evolution

We knew Dr. Macreadie would be very familiar with the fact that the occasional mutation can make it easier for a microbe to survive attack by a particular antibiotic, for example. Since the belief that mutations can add new information is crucial to the idea of microbe-to-man evolution, we asked about this.

He told us, "All you see in the lab is either gene duplications, reshuffling of existing genes, or defective genes (with a loss of information) that might help a bug to survive—say by not being able to bind the drug as effectively. But you never see any new information arising in a cell. Sometimes a bacterium can 'inject' information into another one, so it's 'new' to that bacterium—but that information had to arise somewhere, and we just don't observe it happening. It's hard to see how any serious scientist could believe that real information can arise just by itself, from nothing."

Ian McCreadie acknowledged that being a biblical creationist "has led to a lot of difficulties in dealing with other scientists." Persecution, we asked? "I guess more ridicule," he said. "I think you've got to be selective about when and where to make a stand. Sometimes people in a group are just baiting you, waiting for you to put your neck on the line, and then not always being willing to give you a fair opportunity to present your point of view. Whereas one-on-one gives you more of an opportunity to talk through the issues effectively with people."

We left the conversation greatly encouraged by Dr. Ian Macreadie's stand for God's Word, while doing award-winning science at the highest levels of his profession.

An Eye for Creation

Dr. George Marshall obtained his B.Sc. (Hons) in biology at the University of Strathclyde in 1984. He conducted research into bone marrow cancer at the University of Sheffield for three years until invalided out with a serious, normally incurable illness. He was dramatically healed of this in November 1987, and soon obtained an M.Med.Sci. from Sheffield. He then worked at the University of Manchester before taking up a post at the University of Glasgow in 1988. He obtained his Ph.D. in Ophthalmic Science at Glasgow in 1991 and was elected to chartered biologist (C.Biol.) status and to membership of the Institute of Biology (M.I.Biol.) in 1993. He is now Sir Jules Thorn, Lecturer in Ophthalmic Science.

Dr. George Marshall

Question: Dr. Marshall, you wrote to us to comment on the article "Seeing Back to Front" which appeared in the March-May 1996 issue of *Creation* magazine. What was your comment?

Answer: I point out that the principal reason as to why the eye cannot be regarded as being wired backward (as some evolutionists claim) was hidden in a footnote in your article.

Would you care to elaborate?

The light-detecting structures within photoreceptor cells are located in the stack of discs. These discs are being continually replaced by the formation of new ones at the cell body end of the stack, thereby pushing older discs down the stack. Those discs at the other end of the stack are "swallowed" by a single layer of retinal pigment epithelial (RPE) cells. RPE cells are highly active, and for this they need a very large blood supply — the choroid. Unlike the retina, which is virtually

transparent, the choroid is virtually opaque, because of the vast numbers of red blood cells within it. For the retina to be wired the way that Professor Richard Dawkins suggested would require the choroid to come between the photoreceptor cells and the light, for RPE cells must be kept in intimate contact with both the choroid and photoreceptors to perform their job. Anybody who has had the misfortune of a hemorrhage in front of the retina will testify as to how well red blood cells block out the light.

Then what do you think of the idea that the eye is wired backward?

The notion that the eye was wired backward occurred to me as a 13 year old when studying eye anatomy in a school science class. It took me two years of lecturing on human eye anatomy to realize why the eye is wired the way it is. The idea that the eye is wired backward comes from a lack of knowledge of eye function and anatomy.

How do you react to the notion that the human eye is the product of evolution?

The more I study the human eye, the harder it is to believe that it evolved. Most people see the miracle of sight. I see a miracle of complexity on viewing things at 100,000 times magnification. It is the perfection of this complexity that causes me to baulk at evolutionary theory.

Can you give our readers some idea of just how complex the eye is?

The retina is probably the most complicated tissue in the whole body. Millions of nerve cells interconnect in a fantastic number of ways to form a miniature "brain." Much of what the photoreceptors "see" is interpreted and processed by the retina long before it enters the brain.

A computer program has allegedly "imitated" the evolution of an eye. Do you accept this?

Those who produced this model would acknowledge that the model is such a gross oversimplification that it cannot be cited as a proof. May I quote a colleague's reaction:

"Computer simulation of evolutionary processes such as that described have three important flaws. First, the findings imply that the development which is being measured over so many generations is independent of development of other structures which are necessary for function. Second, the changes observed from the simulation are dependent on the original data input which clearly is consequent to human design of the sequences/regions to be worked on and also the program(s) which are used for the simulation. These are not, therefore, random. The third aspect of all this is that there is translation error in such simulations involving computer hardware/software. This can take the form of electronic error in single bits which are coding for a particular digit. Over many loops in this performance, intrinsic error can be magnified considerably. Was the simulation repeated using different PCs, etc.? One feels that these three arguments are essential to any computer simulation package of evolutionary processes.

"My first point indicated that even if there is an eye, it will be useless unless the organism has the neural and/or the mental processes to utilize information perceived by the eye. How can a chance mutation provide this complexity in several different structures? The argument has usually been that there is a plausible intermediate series of eye-designs in living animals. For example, euglena has an eyespot, other organisms have a "cup" which acts as a direction finder.

"However, the organism which defies this evolution is nautilus. It has a primitive eye with no lens, which is somewhat surprising considering that its close relative, the squid, has one. This organism has (apparently!) been around for millions of years but has never "evolved" a lens, despite the fact that it has a retina which would benefit from this simple change." (Dr. John Hay, B.Sc. (Hons), Ph.D., M.Sc., C.Biol., F.I.Biol.)

What exactly does your work involve?

Lecturing to doctors in medicine who have specialized in ophthalmology and are attempting to gain fellowship with the Royal College of Ophthalmology (FRCOphth). However, my main remit is research into eye diseases using a combination of transmission electron microscopy and immunocytochemistry — a technique that uses antibodies to locate specific proteins such as enzymes.

Do you believe that accepting creation as portrayed in Genesis is essential to your Christian faith?

Yes! On not literally accepting the Genesis account of creation one is left with a major problem — what Scriptures do you accept as true and what Scriptures do you reject as false? Only by accepting the whole of Scripture as the inspired Word of God does one avoid this dilemma. There are Scriptures that are a source of stumbling to the intellect. My practice is to "pigeonhole" them temporarily and never allow them to be a stumbling block to my faith. It's amazing how many of these knotty problems have subsequently resolved themselves. Thus, Genesis creation may initially appear to be hard to accept, but it strikes me that evolution is equally if not more problematic to believe.

How useful do you find *Creation* magazine?

Its principal value is that it challenges what is uncritically accepted. Watch any TV program involving nature and you would think that evolution is an established fact. People get bombarded with this so often that they accept it

(Above left) The retina — probably the most complicated tissue in the whole body. (Above right) Cross-section of the human eye. Dr. Marshall says, "The idea that the eye is wired backward comes from a lack of knowledge of eye function and anatomy."

without thinking. *Creation* magazine makes people realize that it is only a proposal and not fact. There are numerous places in my hospital where I can leave copies on coffee tables to get people to think for themselves.

What advice would you have for Christian students, or for Christians in a science course or teaching situation?

First, recognize that science can become a "religion" in its own right. Scientists say something, so the general public (the "worshipers") accept it without question. Scientists are much more

cautious about one another's findings. Second, science is not static. The science of today is quite different in many ways from the science of yesterday, and will probably bear little resemblance to the science of tomorrow. People once believed in "spontaneous generation" — which could be "proved" by putting

an old sack and a few bits of cheese in a dark corner. Mice spontaneously generated out of the sack. We laugh at such notions, but I suspect that in a hundred years' time people will laugh at some of our scientific notions. Third, one can still become an eminent scientist without accepting evolutionary dogma; the ability to produce sound science in the laboratory is not diminished by one's stance on creation.

Dr. Marshall, thank you very much.

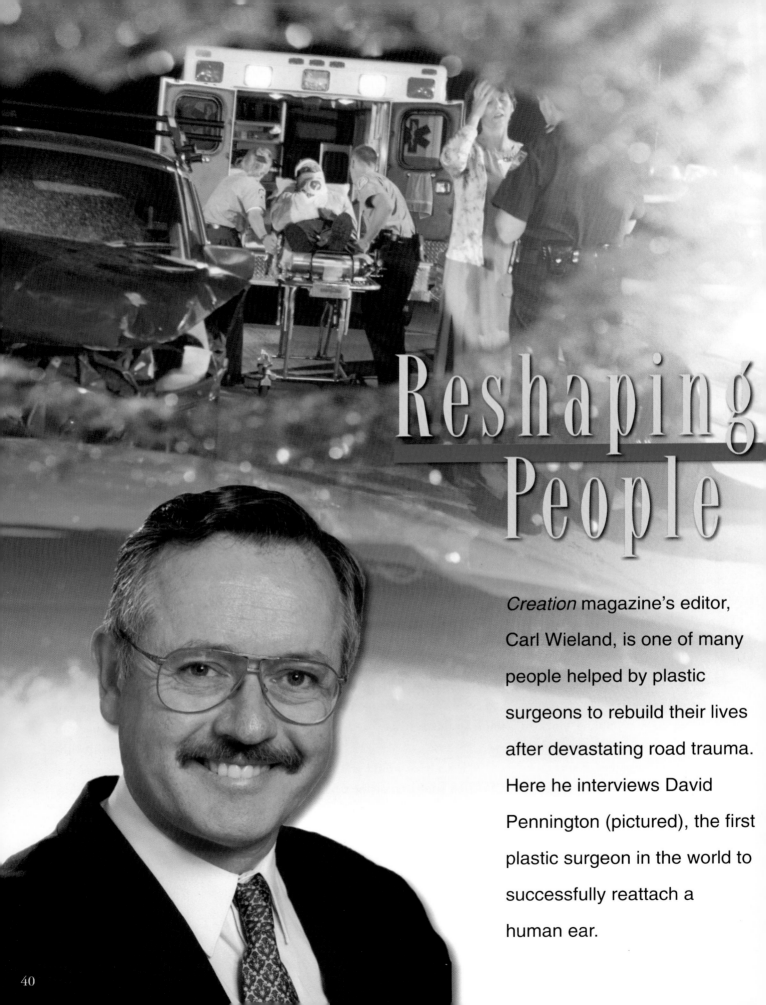

Reshaping People

Creation magazine's editor, Carl Wieland, is one of many people helped by plastic surgeons to rebuild their lives after devastating road trauma. Here he interviews David Pennington (pictured), the first plastic surgeon in the world to successfully reattach a human ear.

CW: Dr. Pennington, why the word "plastic" in front of "surgeon"?

DP: Patients frequently think that I am going to use some sort of molded plastic to fix their faces or whatever. But the word "plastic" has been around a lot longer than the materials we call that today. It comes from the Greek *plassein*, meaning to mold or shape something, which is basically what plastic surgeons do to the body.

Does your work mostly involve making people look better, or repairing damage?

Most of my work is reconstructive surgery, but there is an overlap with the cosmetic. Some people have features they might describe as unfortunate, that they inherited, that cause them psychological upset, where a remolding process will help them in their life. So that would commonly be called cosmetic surgery. My particular interest is in reconstruction of the female breast after it has been removed in cancer surgery.

Using fatty tissue from somewhere else in that person?

Yes. I've been in the forefront of developing what's called the "TRAM flap." A portion of lower abdominal tissue is removed, and the tiny blood vessels which "feed" it are carefully detached and are reattached to small blood vessels in the armpit. The tissue is then shaped to form a breast. As well as having a new breast after

> *"The more you look, and the smaller you look, the more you find. The tiny, tiny things we get down to — the molecules in the cell — are miraculous, just unbelievable."*

losing the old one to cancer, the lady has a flatter tummy.

I gather much of this sort of microsurgical work was pioneered in Australia in the last few decades?

That's right. One can use such techniques to reattach parts of limbs, noses, scalp, ears, and various other parts of the body that have been traumatically severed. Or we can do these things electively. Say we want to reconstruct a part of the body, for example, a face that has been damaged by cancer surgery. We can take a part of the body from elsewhere, and reattach the blood vessels at its new location, so that the part we are moving stays alive.

Please tell us about your "world first" in reattaching an ear.

In 1979, a patient involved in a motor accident came into the Sydney hospital where I was working. Strangely, the only injury he had was that his ear was torn off. I rang the head of the unit and said that I proposed to try to reattach the ear. We were both aware that it had

never been done before. He basically said, "Go for it." Thankfully, it worked.

Why hadn't previous attempts succeeded?

The problem in ears is that the blood vessels are so tiny, about 1/50th of an inch (0.5mm) in diameter, and it's very hard to tell the arteries from the veins, even under the microscope. Now if you join an artery to a vein you've got the plumbing wrong, and it won't work. So we did something new to overcome this problem. We used the vessels that run on the scalp in front of the ear,[1] turning them back to act as an arterial conduit. By attaching this artery to a tiny artery in the ear, and letting it bleed, it was easier to distinguish the veins once the vessels were filled with blood.

Are ears now routinely reattached?

This is a very rare injury, and I think that since 1979 there have been only about 15 subsequent cases in the world literature.

Does anyone ask you, as a Christian, why you are doing corrective surgery; aren't you "interfering with the way God made things"?

Sure. But that applies to virtually all of medicine. Eating the correct diet and keeping fit will decrease your chance of disease, but some diseases happen that are not your fault, that are "unfair." Go back 100 or 200 years: children were

Dr. David Pennington

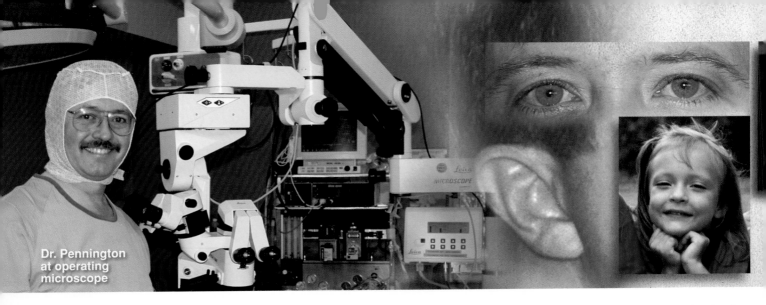

Dr. Pennington at operating microscope

dying like flies from infectious diseases through no fault of theirs. That's where a biblical perspective is important, because this world is not "fair"; it is not the way God made things in the beginning, but due to what happened after that.

You mean the Fall, and the curse on creation when Adam rebelled?

Yes. I believe there was a time when man was created perfect, not susceptible to these sorts of things. When you look into the chemistry and chromosomes, you find evidence of a complex design which is now marred. I believe this is because of what the Bible calls sin.

So we're looking at a fallen creation, which only makes sense when you take Genesis and a recent creation literally.

That's right. If there were millions of years of death and bloodshed before people appeared on the scene, what would be the point of fighting against all these bad things like disease? In that scheme of things, they would just have been part of what God called "very good" [Genesis 1:31]. But how could God proclaim that disease and death were "very good"? That doesn't make

sense, especially when death is called the "last enemy" [1 Corinthians 15:26].

As a doctor, then, when you fight against disease, or reshape someone who is deformed as a result of an inherited mutation, you're really fighting against the effects of that Genesis curse.

Yes, we're fighting a rearguard action in trying to repair the damage that is occurring.

Christ didn't just passively say, "Well, this is the way it is," but actively opposed the effects of the Curse in healing people. Are you in a sense following His example?

That's true. He was the Great Healer — the Bible indicates He probably spent more time healing than preaching.

Has anyone referred to Christ's reattachment[2] of the ear that Peter cut off [John 18:10, Luke 22:49–51] in comparison to your work?

Yes, but it's an uncomfortable comparison. Christ did it with a touch, it took me seven hours.

Are your unbelieving medical colleagues sometimes awed by the design in the human body?

Yes, a lot of these so-called evolutionists are constantly using words like "wonderful" and "design." They are almost unconsciously having to accept that things look marvellously designed. The more you look, and the smaller you look, the more you find. The tiny, tiny things we get down to — the molecules in the cell — are miraculous, just unbelievable. As medical students 30 years ago, we were told, "We don't understand this; we don't understand that . . ." and now that we're understanding some of these things, they are astonishingly more complex than we ever thought.

How does your belief in Genesis creation affect your interaction with your colleagues?

It's difficult working in a world which is almost entirely evolution-believing, but from time to time I can have discussions, and I pass on information which casts doubt on what they have been taught. I find *Creation* magazines to be excellent for this and for teaching in church as well.

We've published evidence[3] exposing some bogus claims about finding such things as Noah's ark, the ark of the covenant, etc. Please share the personal experience you've had concerning this.

Your magazine referred to these people, Ron Wyatt [now deceased] from Tennessee and his disciple [Jonathan Gray], saying they have discovered all these wonderful things that prove the Bible true — including also the Red Sea crossing, Christ's actual blood, and so on. Now it would be marvelous if such claims were true, but if they are false, it will come out, and the world will say, "These are the people who support the Bible and they're telling lies." So it does the Bible no good at all; it is actually anti-Christian, if the results of their speculations cause people to doubt the Scripture. The Bible says we should "prove all things" [1 Thessalonians 5:21].

Why do you think the claims are not true?

First, because whenever the claims are held up to the cold, hard light of scientific day, they are found seriously wanting. Second, there's sufficient evidence that they have not always told the truth. I have personal evidence of that. I attended one of Jonathan Gray's meetings where he made various claims about the ark of the covenant, including the blood of Christ. He said, for instance, that the blood allegedly found on the mercy seat was unique in having no male chromosomal material, but showed complete ignorance of chromosomes by saying it had 22 X chromosomes. This is absurd, and would be incompatible with life — males have one X, females have two.

Did you tell him this?

Yes, I wrote to him about this and other inconsistencies and errors, and he wrote back skipping about the issues and unsuccessfully trying to justify himself. I more or less left the matter, until, a couple of years later, I was told I was featured in his book. He refers to a "Dr. P.D." who, despite the reversed initials, is obviously me, as he actually quotes *verbatim* from my letter. He makes it appear that he comes out on top while having a face to face discussion with me, and describes "Dr. P.D." as "sitting there seething" and words to that effect. But it is a **total fabrication** — there was no such meeting or conversation. This is clearly deceptive, and indicates that the man deals lightly with the truth. I have other careful eyewitness reports of similar instances.

Is there anything you would like to leave with readers?

Both my sons are Christians and at college. They're facing the continual attacks from evolutionists that Christians in the biological sphere face. The material from *Answers in Genesis* is incredibly helpful, especially the way it is based on starting from the Word of God. Because you can argue till the cows come home about the science, ultimately it boils down to evolution being a faith and Christianity a faith. Without a strong Christian faith, you're not going to be able to stand against the evolutionary arguments.

Dr. Pennington, thanks very much.

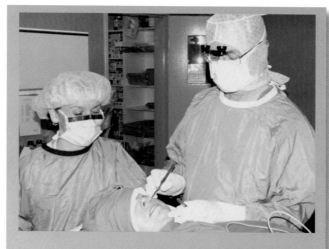

". . . a biblical perspective is important, because this world is not 'fair'; it is not the way God made things in the beginning. . . ."

References and notes

1. The superficial temporal artery and vein.
2. This miracle of instant healing may have involved the creation of a new ear; we are not told.
3. A.A. Snelling, "Amazing 'Ark' Exposé," Creation 14(4):26–38, 1992; "Has the Ark of the Covenant Been Found?" *Creation* 21(2):10–14, 1999.

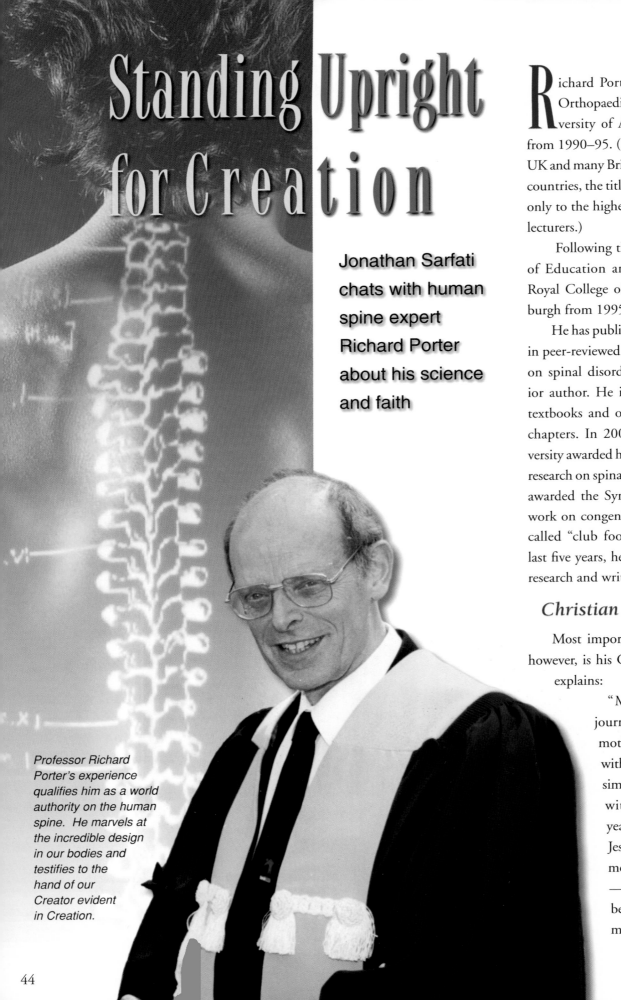

Standing Upright for Creation

Jonathan Sarfati chats with human spine expert Richard Porter about his science and faith

Professor Richard Porter's experience qualifies him as a world authority on the human spine. He marvels at the incredible design in our bodies and testifies to the hand of our Creator evident in Creation.

Richard Porter was Professor of Orthopaedic Surgery at the University of Aberdeen, Scotland, from 1990–95. (In universities in the UK and many British Commonwealth countries, the title "Professor" is given only to the highest rank of university lecturers.)

Following that, he was Director of Education and Training for the Royal College of Surgeons of Edinburgh from 1995–97.

He has published over 120 papers in peer-reviewed journals (50 percent on spinal disorders), mostly as senior author. He is the author of five textbooks and over 30 contributory chapters. In 2001, Edinburgh University awarded him a D.Sc. degree for research on spinal stenosis, and he was awarded the Syme professorship for work on congenital talipes (formerly called "club foot"). Retired for the last five years, he still continues with research and writing.

Christian commitment

Most important to Prof. Porter, however, is his Christian faith, as he explains:

"My own spiritual journey began when my mother and father shared with me the way to find a simple close relationship with the Lord. At 11 years of age, I accepted Jesus personally — life's most important choice — and I have never been disappointed. My main objective is to encourage others to know Jesus and experience the new life of the indwelling Holy Spirit — that is, the new birth.

"Because of the amazing miracle of God coming to us in Jesus — miraculously conceived by the Holy Spirit, born of the virgin Mary — and rising from the dead (which doesn't usually happen!) — the whole thinking of a Christian is inevitably quite different from that of an unbeliever."

Asked about the Book of Genesis, Prof. Porter replied, "It makes sense that because we are children of a loving God, who has shown himself in Jesus, then a literal understanding of the early chapters of Genesis (that God chose to create that way) is no problem. It was clearly the way Jesus read it (Matthew 19:3–6, Mark 10:6–9)."

With his record of scientific papers and awards, Prof. Porter would have to smile at those who claim that no creationist publishes in the scientific literature or does real research. Some evolutionists, forced by such indisputable facts to grudgingly admit that some creationists do real research, try the tack that such creationists are really using evolutionary, not creationist, principles in their research. On the contrary, Richard says, "It is just the opposite. A person who begins with the premise that God has made an excellent design is at an advantage — he is able to ask questions that the evolutionist never thought about. The most important thing in research is to begin by asking the right question."

Back pain versus evolution

Richard pointed out that evolutionary theory can be unproductive for research: "For example, the curve of the lumbar spine toward the front — the lordosis — was thought by evolutionists to be a problem, the result of man having recently adopted an upright position. So, some researchers blamed back pain on this, saying the spine had not yet evolved satisfactorily. If

therapists have the wrong starting assumption, then it's not surprising that treatments for lordosis are unhelpful. If a spine fracture causes a lumbar kyphosis (curvature in the opposite direction), that spine is significantly weakened."[1]

He added that the creationist perspective has always been foundational to his research: "I start from quite a different position. From my understanding of human anatomy and physiology and my understanding of God, I say that the form of God's creation always matches its function. So you can be sure that the form of the spine is perfectly designed for its function. God has made a wonderful spine. If you start with that premise, it gives you a head start when trying to understand the mechanism of the spine.

"When you start to examine the biomechanics of the curved spine, asking why it's that shape, and what's good about it, you find that the arch of the spine has a beautiful purpose. Like the arch of a bridge, it adds strength. Because of that arch in the lumbar spine, a person with a lumbar lordosis can lift proportionally more weight than a gorilla with its kyphotic (opposite curvature) spine! So it's not surprising that treating back pain with postures and exercises that *restore* the lordosis works exceedingly well."[2]

The splendid spine

Since the spine is his specialty field, he could tell us about more of its amazing features: "My inaugural lecture in Aberdeen was 'Upright Man,' and I tried to explain how the wonderful human spine is a perfect match between form and function. Things go wrong with the spine when we abuse it (if we fail to keep ourselves fit, or overload it, or have an accident). We are learning to use 'foam filling' in building (a sandwich of honeycomb material between two plates) to make something that is both light and strong, but the bones of the spine have been 'foam filled' with cancellous bone (with an open, latticed, or porous structure), surrounded by harder cortical bone, since the creation.

"The vertebral bodies increase in cross-sectional area as you go farther down the spine, because in the upright position, the lower ones take more load. The bones are not denser, just bigger. By contrast, animals that walk on all fours have a roughly horizontal spine that is equally loaded all the way. So all their vertebrae are of similar cross-sectional area. Form matches function. If evolutionists were right in saying we had recently attained upright posture, our vertebral bodies should be like those of quadrupeds, but they are not.

"We designed radial-ply tires for motor cars, but God constructed the rim of the intervertebral disc with radial-ply fibers from the beginning. That construction makes a healthy disc stronger than the bones. When one examines the way the human body is formed and how it works, one is constantly amazed. It's like looking at a piece of beautiful bone china and seeing the maker's mark beneath."[3]

More creationist contributions to medicine

The contributions of modern creationists to scientific research are well-kept secrets by the modern media and scientific establishment, but Prof. Porter is not the only one. He talks about a leading pathologist:

"Denis Burkitt was a good friend with an inquiring mind. In Africa, as a missionary surgeon, he constantly asked questions, and noticed a lymphoma [a type of cancer] localized to certain parts of Central and East Africa. With only a £50 ($91.77) grant, he visited many mission hospitals and mapped the geographic location of the disease. He then correctly deduced that the tumor was caused by a mosquito-borne virus. This tumor, the first recognized as having a viral origin, is now known as Burkitt's Lymphoma.

"Denis also won *world* acclaim for observing links between many killer diseases of the Western world and lack of fiber in our diet. He was responsible, more than anyone else, for Westerners turning to a high fiber diet. He was also a great man of God who took the Bible at face value. He believed that God has spoken the truth in Genesis."

The "age" question

We find that an increasing number of Christians are rejecting biological evolution in favor of direct creation, but some still balk at taking the time scale literally. Prof. Porter counsels:

"We can look at cosmic and biological science and say perhaps that sometimes the observations don't *seem* to fit Genesis, but wait a bit — there are lots of suppositions. Keep thinking, and you can be confident that eventually science will show God did it the way He said He did.

"Different scientists may examine the same facts about biology, geology, or cosmology but reach quite different conclusions. The evolutionist will reach one view probably because he never thinks about, or rejects, a young earth.

"I'm greatly encouraged that an increasing number of scientists seem to be accepting a straightforward reading of Genesis. Even though the number

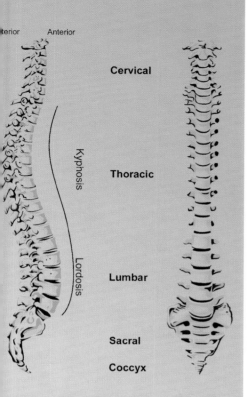

Cervical

Thoracic

Kyphosis

Lordosis

Lumbar

Sacral

Coccyx

Anterior

INJURY STATISTICS

Our human spine is among the most ingeniously designed structures to be found anywhere. In this fallen world, it is estimated that 70–90% of all people in the US will suffer at least one back injury in their lives. Up to 25% become chronic. Much of this is exacerbated by failure to keep the surrounding muscles strong.

actually carrying out research in that framework is small, it is exciting to see the number of insights that have arisen, and models that have been developed that seem to show how the facts fit Genesis exceedingly well. So even though there is a long way to go, the creationist is asking the right question and keeps thinking, whereas the evolutionist stops asking the right question. So in the search for truth, it is the creationist who is likely to come up with the right answers.

"Many of the discrepancies between evolutionists and creationists revolve around our concept of time. My hunch is we are going to find that there is more than one time frame. The issue is not ultimately the observations of the earth sciences, but the conclusions the evolutionists have drawn from them."[4]

Advice for students

When he was a professor in Aberdeen, Richard led what colleagues said was a highly productive research unit, and he enjoyed helping to train young surgeons. He says, "We need lots of young people who love the Lord to make a career in science, including biological science. They will discover that God's thoughts, which match His revealed Word, are written into creation. For too long I think Darwinism has undermined confidence in God's Word — the good news of His eternal salvation, which is available to everyone who turns to Him in Christ."

Prof. Porter with part of his family—wife Christine, and son Matthew with his wife Samantha and their sons Luke, Ben and Joel.

Family life

Professor Porter's family is very important to him. He and his wife, Christine, have four adult sons and nine little grandchildren. The eldest son is a senior lecturer in orthopedics, the second a Methodist minister with a heart for revival, the third an Anglican vicar in a growing church, and the fourth is a doctor, now in training for the Anglican ministry. Prof. Porter says, "My wife and I are just so thrilled that our sons, whether doctors or preachers of the gospel, share in the one ministry. The main thing for us all is to be serving God wherever we are."

References and notes

1. See also J. Bergman, "Back Problems: How Darwinism Misled Researchers," *TJ* 15(3):79–84, 2001.

2. R. Smail, "Oh, My Aching Back!" "*Creation* 12(4):20–21: September 1990. New Zealand physiotherapist Robin McKenzie discovered this lordosis-restoring treatment by chance in 1956. While not a creationist, McKenzie's work lends considerable support to creation.

3. See also C. Wieland, "Adam's Rib: Creation & the Human Body," *Answers in Genesis*, 2001.

4. Nuclear physicist Dr. Russell Humphreys has a variant on this idea, using the well-documented principle of Einstein's general relativity that gravity slows time. See the *Starlight and Time* book and video available from AiG.

PROFESSING CREATION

Dr Walter J. Veith, B.Sc. (Hons), M.Sc. (cum laude), Ph.D., was at the time of interview a (full) professor at the University of the Western Cape (Republic of South Africa) where he held the chair of zoology.

Ours is an age of incessant pro-evolution media tub-thumping. Some have even declared that "all of biology" depends on the truth of evolution. So it was refreshing to talk to Professor Veith (pronounced "fight"), a zoologist of the highest academic rank, who is firmly convinced of the truth of biblical creation.

When we asked how he became a Christian, he said, "It's a long story, but I was an evolutionist, and an atheist. I started to get interested in the subject of biblical prophecy—for example, prophecies in the Book of Daniel, chapter two. They were written long before the events portrayed there, and the kingdoms came in succession just as it says. And the Dead Sea Scrolls seemed to confirm the authenticity and antiquity of the Book of Daniel. So I started to get interested in the rest of Scripture, including Genesis."

Dr. Veith said that he had already been undergoing some "evolution" himself—he started off as a classical Darwinian "gradualist," believing that evolution happened by the slow accumulation of little changes. But because the fossil record does not show creatures gradually changing into others, he was drawn to the later idea that evolution must have happened "in spurts and bursts." He noticed also that evolutionists were conceding that in the so-called Cambrian rocks, supposedly not long after the dawn of multi-celled life, "even the chordates were there before they were supposed to be. Articles were appearing in the literature about 'explosive evolution' in the Cambrian, in which there were already chordates, the phylum to which man belongs. So basically it was just one logical step to believing in Creation."

Natural selection

There were other problems with evolutionary theory to which Walter Veith's training and experience alerted him. For instance, natural selection. He said, "The very name

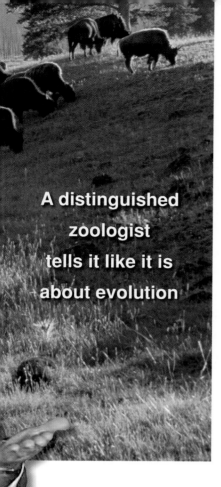

A distinguished zoologist tells it like it is about evolution

'selection' implies that you're choosing between two or more variants. So that means that the end result is extinction of one in favor of the other.

"Natural selection never increases the number of variants, it only decreases them. So my problem with it was, 'How does a mechanism that makes less and less end up making more and more?'

"The answer obviously is, it doesn't. That leaves chance mutations as the only source of the new information. You have to have all these new genes coding for new features, all interacting precisely with one another, continually arising as animals get more complex, by chance. To believe that, you have to have a lot of faith. It's

certainly not something I see in my work as a zoologist."

Some fascinating comments by Dr. Veith concerned the tremendous built-in ability of some animals to adapt to changing conditions, much too rapidly to have anything to do with any proposed evolutionary mechanisms or millions of years. For example, island deer have been seen to respond to a scarcity of resources by decreasing their body size by as much as two-thirds. "Naked mole rats," he also pointed out, "if the ecological circumstances get tough, respond with a whole host of drastic rearrangements of their genetic material, so-called 'jumping genes' doing their thing. This creates a far greater variety in the offspring, which of course has an effect on selection.

"I think that organisms were endowed with a great capacity for variation, and that we haven't begun to figure out all the mechanisms in the latent DNA. Evolutionists have tried to write this DNA off as leftover 'junk,' but it is increasingly recognized as playing an important (though still largely unknown) role."

After the Flood

We asked Prof. Veith whether such built-in mechanisms for rapid variation could be the remnants of mechanisms from the original kinds which, after the Flood, enabled populations such as the original "dog kind"

to rapidly diversify into wolves, coyotes, dingoes, etc.

"Absolutely," he replied. "A lot of the rearrangement can simply come about by playing different tunes on the same piano, as it were. There are organisms where there appears to have been a fusion of chromosomes, but basically the same information is there, just the order in which it is arranged is different, which has tremendous effects on the organisms themselves."[1]

So what happened after he became a believer in creation? "When I started lecturing to my students (about creation evidences) at my previous university," said Dr. Veith, "it caused havoc, and I had to leave because of it."

How about the present university? "It's still very secular and evolutionistic, but it's much more tolerant of other views. They're a bit reticent to let me lecture on the question of evolution, but I get opportunities to put the counter view. The occasional creation/evolution lecture after hours is normally well attended and appreciated. The students here tend to have more religious roots, so they are not as evolutionarily inclined. We have a large number of the previously disadvantaged community, and when people have been through tough times like they have, there tend to be closer ties with God."

Zoology

Dr. Walter Veith

49

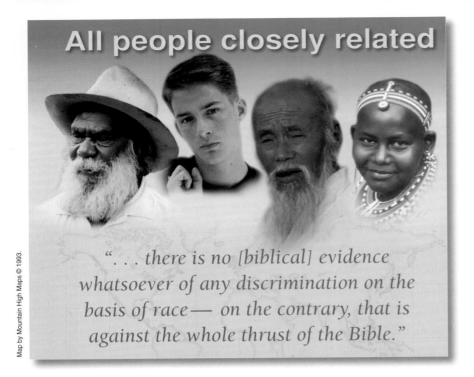

All people closely related

"... there is no [biblical] evidence whatsoever of any discrimination on the basis of race— on the contrary, that is against the whole thrust of the Bible."

Map by Mountain High Maps © 1993.

Racism

Here was an obvious opportunity to raise the subject of apartheid, etc. Dr. Veith agreed totally that if people had taken the Genesis history of mankind seriously, they would have realized that we are all closely related, anyway, so the differences between "races" must be trivial (which is now confirmed by genetic and molecular studies). He said, "The paradigm of evolution (even in its pre-Darwinian manifestations) is one of the root causes of racism."

We asked him about the way in which some in the former South African regime had actually tried to base their racism on the Bible. Dr. Veith replied, "Yes, and that is a gross distortion of the Scriptures. My Bible tells me that God made all people from one man [Acts 17:26] and that the gospel is for every nation, tribe, and people [Revelation 14:6].

"Some even used the account in Genesis about the 'curse on Ham' to justify discrimination," he said. "But it

was not on Ham, but on Canaan [Genesis 9:25–26], and there is no evidence whatsoever of any discrimination on the basis of race—on the contrary, that is against the whole thrust of the Bible."

Animals without death?

With his experience in ecological matters, we asked Dr. Veith about a common argument raised against the clear biblical teaching that death and bloodshed among animals[2] only commenced after the fall of Adam; that is, that looking at today's world, it appears that one needs death in order to have a finely balanced food chain.

"But that's looking at what we have today, not what we had in the beginning," he replied. "We only have a

"The geologists were so furious they exploded and called me a liar, [and said] that such research had never been done."

fraction of the flora and fauna that were there at first—the fossil record bears that out. We don't know what animals ate in the past. Tooth structure is not a good indicator. The panda bear is classified on the basis of its tooth structure as a carnivore, but it eats bamboo. An animal that has the tools for the original diet may also find them suitable for a more carnivorous diet if a need arose. There are many examples of that. With the destruction of northern hemisphere forests by acid rain, for instance, animals like chipmunks, normally seed-eaters, will now eat animals run over on the road.

"New Zealand's kea parrots started to attack and eat sheep. They have the same talons and beak structure as a bird of prey but weren't using them for this until their food source ran out. And most bears—even fish are only eaten by them at the time of the salmon run, because there are no berries around in that early season. Later, they become 70–80 percent herbivore, even though they have the 'equipment' to be carnivorous.

"Even the venom apparatus in snakes may have been used to inject an enzyme to soften food. So, many things may not necessarily have been designed for killing other animals. But it does indicate in the Bible that God restructured some organisms.

"I think He used the existing genetic material and just reorganized the way it was expressed. For instance, a thorn is a modified leaf, just curled tightly upon itself. So the gene didn't necessarily change; the way in which it was expressed changed. Or perhaps some latent genetic information switched on after the Fall."

Playing God

Dr. Veith's current research appears to be showing that herbivorous animals fed with large amounts of animal protein are in danger of osteoporosis from excess calcium excretion.[3] He said, "They lock up these animals and feed them anything from edible plastic to manure and ground-up animals. That's one of the factors behind the spread of mad cow disease,[4] one of the things I am working on. People treat farm animals like commodities, because they think they are just chance accumulations of evolved genes. So if you think an animal doesn't have everything it should have, why not just play God, and take a couple of genes from something else and add them? Animals were also created for man's pleasure and companionship, not as mere food factories. Today, there is, of course, also the opposite side of the evolutionary coin, the animal rights movement, which elevates animals to the level of humans, since all are seen as just chance evolved entities."

We asked him if, in the light of man's dominion mandate over other creatures in Genesis, he would have problems with all forms of "genetic engineering" in animals. He said, "No. But I would have a major problem transplanting genes that totally changed the physiology. For example transgenic pigs, where the gene for human growth hormone is engineered into pigs. You get very large pigs, but they are also incredibly diseased — because these are not 'add-on' genes, they alter something integral to the normal developmental process of the animal.

"You need proper research to be able to make the decisions as to where to draw the line."

Dr. Veith is also convinced about the evidence for a young world, and a global Flood. He said, "I gave a lecture at the University of Cape Town once, and presented the evidence from my slides that the famous Yellowstone petrified 'forests' were not a succession of separate forests over vast ages, but were the result of a catastrophic event.[5]

"The geologists were so furious they exploded and called me a liar, that such research had never been done. Knowing where it had been published, I asked them, 'What journal would you like it to be published in?' They said, 'If it was in something like the *Journal of Paleontology* it would have been acceptable.' I said, 'That's exactly where it is, and you'll have a copy on your desk.'[6] So I sent them a copy, with the article by a creationist scientist. And the next day they came back and said, 'But it says nothing about a worldwide Flood.' I said, 'Exactly. If it said it was a world Flood, nobody would ever publish it. But it's clear that these logs were deposited by massive catastrophism.' "

We asked Dr. Veith for a final comment to leave with readers. He said, "Read Genesis just as it stands. There's a lot of evidence to favor the words written there. For evolution and long ages, there's nothing but propped-up theories that have to be re-propped and re-propped every so often to be maintained. But God's Word is timeless."

References and notes

1. Since no new information is added, this has nothing to do with "fish to philosopher" evolution, for which one needs processes capable of adding new information.

2. Only creatures which have the *nephesh* ("soul" or psyche) have life in the way in which the Bible refers to it. So plants, for example, may "die" biologically, but do not die in the biblical sense. The same is probably true for bacteria, fungi, and perhaps even insects.

3. This calciuresis appears to be caused by the fact that animal protein has more sulfur-containing amino acids.

4. The disease can be spread when infected animals are ground up as part of the feed for other cattle.

5. J. Sarfati, "The Yellowstone Petrified Forests," *Creation* 21(2)18–21 (1999).

6. H.G. Coffin, "Orientation of Trees in the Yellowstone Petrified Forests," *Journal of Paleontology* 50(3):539–543 (1976).

PHYSICAL SCIENCES

"In the beginning, O Lord, you laid the foundations of the earth, and the heavens are the work of your hands.— Hebrews 1:10

John Baumgardner (B.S., M.S., Ph.D (UCLA) is a geophysicist employed at the Los Alamos National Laboratory in New Mexico. His work involves detailed computer modeling of the structure and processes of the earth's interior, as well as a variety of other fluid dynamics phenomena.

Probing the Earth's
DEEP PLACES

Carl Wieland and Don Batten interview plate tectonics* expert Dr. John Baumgardner

Question: Dr. Baumgardner, some say that because of continental drift (the idea that the continents have broken apart and moved thousands of miles) one has to believe in "millions of years."

JB: Well, I believe there is now overwhelming evidence in favor of continental breakup and large-scale plate tectonic* activity. The acceptance of these concepts is an amazing example of a scientific revolution, which occurred roughly between 1960 and 1970. However, this revolution did not go far enough, because the earth science community neglected and suppressed the evidences for catastrophism — large-scale, rapid change — throughout the geological record. So the time scale the uniformitarian scientists today are using is dramatically too long. The strong weight of evidence is that there was a massive catastrophe, corresponding to the Genesis flood, which involved large and rapid continental movements. My conclusion is that the only mechanism capable of producing that scale of catastrophe and not wrecking the planet in the process had to be internal to the earth.

*Plate tectonics: *The concept that the earth's outer shell consists of separate, huge "plates" on which the continents ride, capable of movement relative to one another.*

I am persuaded it involved rapid subduction (sinking) of the pre-Flood ocean floor, pulling the "plates" apart at the beginning of the Flood, and was probably associated with the breaking up of the "fountains of the great deep" described in Scripture.

A 1993 *New Scientist* article spoke highly of your 3-D supercomputer model of plate tectonics.[1]

There are to my knowledge three other computer codes for modelling the earth's mantle and so on, in the world. These other three use a mathematical method not so well suited for the modern parallel supercomputers. The one I developed uses the finite element technique and performs very well on the new, very large supercomputers. So, many of my colleagues are recognizing it as the most capable code in the world. Last year NASA funded this effort as one of the nine grand challenge projects for the next three years in their High Performance Computing and Communication initiative, and are supporting two post-doctoral researchers to collaborate with me to improve it, and apply it to study the earth.

This code is comparable to what are called general circulation models for the atmosphere and oceans, which are some of the largest codes in the world in terms of how much machine power they consume. It's got lots of physics in it to model the details of the mechanical behavior of the silicate rock inside the earth. My present focus is to make the representation of the tectonic plates even more realistic. So the code is in an ongoing state of development, but it's come a long way in the last 15 years.

We understand you've shown that as these floating blocks of rock push down into the material below, things get hotter, so the "slipperyness" increases and there's a runaway effect. The faster they sink, the hotter they get, so the faster they can sink.

Yes — rock that represents the ocean floor is colder, and therefore denser than the rock below it and so can sink into the earth's interior. And the properties of the rock inside the earth, especially at the high temperatures that exist there, make it possible for the colder rock from the earth's surface to peel away and sink in a runaway manner down through the mantle — very rapidly.

So this "happens" on your computer model all by itself, from the laws of science — over a short time scale, not millions of years?

That's correct. Exactly how long is something I'm working to refine. But it seems that once this sinking of the pre-Flood ocean floor (in a conveyor-belt-like fashion down into the earth, pulling things apart behind it) starts, it is not a slow process spanning millions of years — it's almost certain that it runs to completion and "recycles" all of the existing floor in a few weeks or months.

You're part of a team of top creation scientists[2] **which is developing a model of catastrophic plate tectonics based on this mechanism, which believes the continents broke up (from a single landmass) during, not after the Flood as some have proposed.**

Yes. There is compelling evidence from the fossil-bearing sediments on the continents that the breakup occurred during the time these sediments were being deposited. We are convinced that this "continental sprint," as it's been called, was during the time of the Flood, and part of the mechanism for it.

In his hand are the depths of the earth, and the mountain peaks belong to him. – Psalm 95:4

Dr. John Baumgardner

55

How did you become a Christian?

Primarily through a verse-by-verse Bible study in the Gospel of John, in a college Sunday school class when I was 26 years old. It focused on the question of who is this Jesus Christ, and is He authentic or not? I had little church background prior to that point, but a lot of scientific training. I was well schooled in evolution, and it took several months before I started to realize the problems with this idea. Later, I was exposed to the evidence for a young earth and realized that the case for it was indeed solid.

Why is six-day, recent creation important?

I believe it's a pivotal issue in regard to the reliability of God's Word. It ultimately bears on the authenticity of Jesus, because Jesus put His stamp of authority on the writings of Moses, which, taken at face value, indicate that the original earth was a perfect world, one which included man and woman, one in which there was no death. There were no carnivorous animals — all the animals and man were given the green plants to eat. To make sense of the history of the world as the Bible lays it out, does not allow for millions of years, but does require that there be a catastrophe which destroyed all the air-breathing land life except for that preserved on Noah's ark. So I believe there is no negotiation possible on this question.

So did your current interest in plate tectonics and continental drift arise out of your Christian faith?

Entirely. I recognized that this was probably one of the most burning Bible apologetics issues in my century, and, as far as I could see, there was no one working on it. I sensed the call of

Seafloor "zebra-stripes" don't mean slow and gradual

The mid-ocean "ridges" are undersea mountain chains with volcanoes at the boundary between two "plates" of the earth's outer shell. It is believed that here, molten magma from below can well up as the plates move apart, making new oceanic crust — a process called "sea floor spreading." As the new crust cools down, it "freezes" within it the direction of the earth's magnetic field at that time.

When instruments measuring magnetism are towed (on the ocean surface) across these ridges, they detect bands of alternating magnetic direction, like a "zebra stripe" pattern, with each side of the ridge mirroring the other. This is interpreted to mean that as new sea floor

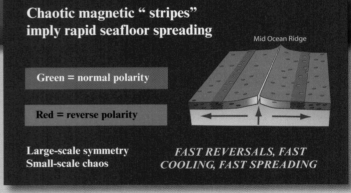

Chaotic magnetic " stripes" imply rapid seafloor spreading

Mid Ocean Ridge

Green = normal polarity

Red = reverse polarity

Large-scale symmetry
Small-scale chaos

FAST REVERSALS, FAST COOLING, FAST SPREADING

had gradually formed on each side of the ridge, the earth's magnetism had slowly reversed many times, over millions of years. However, Dr. Baumgardner says this pattern does not mean the spreading was slow. He says, "From an estimate of the viscosity of the outer core, where the currents associated with the earth's magnetism exist, there is no reason why the magnetic field can't reverse rapidly. Moreover, there is field evidence that it *has* reversed rapidly, within weeks."[3] In addition, drilling the sea floor has shown that, regardless of the overall direction of the magnetism detected from the surface, the magnetic direction within a drill core frequently varies widely.[4] This is less consistent with slow spreading than with a rapid welling up of new magna during a period of rapid reversals; the magma in contact with the surface will reflect the direction at that time, but by the time the deeper magma cools a few weeks later, the direction has switched again — and so on for deeper levels.

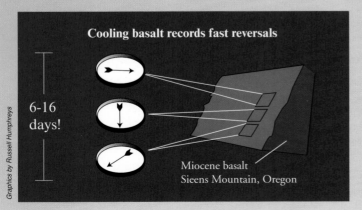

Cooling basalt records fast reversals

6-16 days!

Miocene basalt
Sieens Mountain, Oregon

God, actually. While giving lectures on creation/evolution at college, I realized one of the biggest deficiencies in the creationist position was this lack of an alternative geological model, in particular one accounting for large-scale tectonics. I was 34 when I went back to get a Ph.D. in a field that I previously had not had a single course in. I believe Christians with scientific talent need to be encouraged — just like they're encouraged to become missionaries — to go and get the credentials and the training they need, and work at a professional level in these fields. God has opened incredible doors for me and others.

We published a careful exposé of the claims made by a Ron Wyatt, and more recently by one Jonathan Gray, concerning an alleged "ark site" — an almond-shaped formation in eastern Turkey. In trying to attack our articles, they often quote statements from you supporting this possibly being the ark site. This was before your research at the site caused you to definitely conclude this could not be the ark. They say you now oppose their claims for fear of losing your job.

Ron's claims here are just as bogus as his claims about that site. Far from hiding my creationism, I'm well known for it (especially through letters in the local newspaper) in this scientific community, which has more Ph.D.s per capita than any other place in the United States. My employer and my colleagues know exactly where I stand.

You gave a poster presentation on this "runaway rapid continental drift" mechanism at the American

Geophysical Union meeting in 1994, so at least some of the 6,000 scientists there would have seen it. What was the feedback?

Many people were interested in the numerical techniques I used for such a calculation, because it's a significant computational challenge. Almost no one seemed to appreciate the implications of it. Actually, this concept of "runaway subduction" [rapid sinking of the "plates" as described earlier] has been in the literature for over 30 years. It was picked up in the geophysical community in the early 1970s, but for some reason the interest disappeared. People in my field are not ignorant of this possibility; it's just not seriously explored.

Why do you think that is?

Well, there's no real motivation to pursue it. Some toyed with the idea that such runaway effects might have been involved in recent volcanism in the southwestern United States. But in their framework, they're not really looking for worldwide effects.

So their framework of thinking is really like blinders, preventing a full consideration of all the relevant evidence?

That's correct, exactly. The same kind of uniformitarian "glasses" prevent them from giving much attention to the evidences for catastrophism in the sedimentary record. Such basic philosophical biases profoundly affect the way science approaches problems and weighs the evidence. So it's not simply "facts speaking for themselves" — the framework one starts from can and does

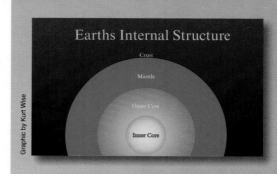

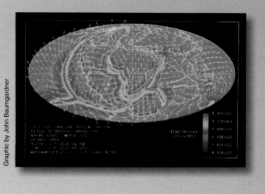

profoundly affect the conclusions that are drawn.

Dr. Baumgardner, thank you very much.

References and notes

1. "How a Supercontinent Went to Pieces," *New Scientist* (January 16, 1993): p. 19.

2. In alphabetical order: Drs. Steve Austin, John Baumgardner, Russell Humphreys, Andrew Snelling, Larry Vardiman, Kurt Wise — sometimes affectionately known as the "Gang of Six." Note that the chapter on continental drift in CSF's *The Answers Book* (one of the co-authors of which is a member of this team) is being modified, in the light of many new findings, for future editions.

3. R.S. Coe, M. Prevot, and P. Camps, "New Evidence for Extraordinarily Rapid Change of the Geomagnetic Field During a Reversal," *Nature* 374:687–692 (April 20, 1995). The finding (by highly respected experts in paleomagnetism) of "astonishing" rates of reversal, has now been duplicated more than once.

4. J.M. Hall and P.T. Robinson, "Deep Crustal Drilling in the North Atlantic Ocean," *Science* 204:573-586 (1980).

> "... for many years I just lived in a world that was sort of split, where there was a church thing and another life — a scientific life. . . ."

MINING FOR THE TRUTH

Carl Wieland interviews geologist Jim Farquhar

Jim Farquhar, B.Sc., M.Sc., is a geologist who has worked in the mining industry in Zimbabwe, South Africa, and Australia, for some 35 years. He has been employed by companies exploring for, and mining, gold, platinum, zinc, lead, copper, and iron ore.

His master of science degree, for a thesis in geological data processing, was awarded by the University of New South Wales in 1998. He currently lives in Western Australia, where he works for Hamersley Iron, part of the large Rio Tinto group.

Jim is well known to me for his work as a volunteer with the Western Australian Support Group of *Answers in Genesis*. His geological expertise has often been invaluable in answering audience questions, as well as being an encouragement to people who have been led to believe that geologists would "obviously" not believe what the Bible so clearly teaches about a young earth and a world Flood.

When we met recently during his visit to our Brisbane office, Jim told me that he had been raised in a very strong Christian home, but to him it was just a lot of formality.

He said, "I first realized that there was a bit more to this Christianity when I was about 14, at a Billy Graham Crusade in Zimbabwe (then Rhodesia). I put my hand up with all the others, but that was it, nothing much really happened after that, until I was about 26, living in South Africa. My wife and I went to a Presbyterian church, and the elderly preacher (he couldn't

preach well at all, but he was a lovely guy) started Bible studies with us. Then I realized again what being a Christian was all about, and he led me through that, and I went home and shared it with my wife, Hilary. She was then not particularly interested, but she also 'broke down' and we both became Christians about that time."

Jim had already been working in the mining industry for some time, and just accepted the "standard view" about the millions

of years. He happened to pick up and read the classic *The Genesis Flood*, by John Whitcomb and Henry Morris.[1] He said, "I realized that there was more to it than I had thought; possibly the Earth was a lot younger than I had been taught. But that was all there was available, and these American creationists seemed so far away, so for many years I just lived in a world that was sort of split, where there was a church thing and another life — a scientific life, a mining life. But then years later, when we were living in Australia, I came across the work of *Answers in Genesis*. They were putting on a weekend seminar, featuring their own Dr. Don Batten, and two American guests, Drs. Don DeYoung and Marvin Lubenow.

"I couldn't believe it"

"I remember asking Don Batten at one of the breaks, 'So what about this classification scheme of living things? We're all linked together; isn't the tree of evolution obvious?' His brief answer showed me that there might be another way of seeing things, so I thought I'd better have another look."

Jim and Hilary Farquhar

Jim told me that he was "really stunned" by the "tables full of books" available at that seminar. He said, "I couldn't believe it. Seeing all the materials makes one realize that it's not just three or four people somewhere in the world, it's hundreds and hundreds of scientists that are believing it. Can they all be wrong? We bought a whole bunch of stuff then, and haven't looked back." Knowing what the materials did in his life, Jim well understands the reason why the AiG ministry has such an emphasis on books and materials. He willingly helps transport many cartons of books to places where an AiG speaker or film is featured.

Jim Farquhar realizes that "the truth and authority of the Bible" is ultimately *the* major issue in Christianity, and that the major Christian doctrines are logically grounded in a literal, historical Genesis. He is excited when he talks about seeing "heaps"[2] of evidence for Noah's flood "everywhere." He told me, "If we look at what happens today in even small localized flooding, then read the Bible and what it says about the Flood and its immensity, it's more than feasible for that Flood to have caused all these huge deposits of sediments we see.

"Once we realize that fossils are not millions of years old, but mainly a record of God's judgment on sin, then there is no record of death and bloodshed before Adam's fall. Suddenly it makes sense when the Bible talks of a once-perfect world, ruined by sin."

Taking the Bible at face value also means a 6–7,000 year time span since creation. To Jim, realizing this truth has been immensely exciting. He pointed out that this meant that one's own potential life span of 70 years was about 1 percent of the lifetime of the whole universe, which brought God that much closer. He said, "It makes life more meaningful. Because prior to that, your life is just a spot, and it's insignificant. But since the world's age is that much shorter, then each person's life has more value."

No need for millions of years

I asked Jim, with his extensive experience in mining, about the anti-creationist claim that if the millions-of-years belief weren't true, mining companies couldn't find ore bodies. He replied, "The only reason that these presumed 'ages' are used in the industry is to give a correlation of rocks, to be able to say these rocks

belong to a certain group, which is more, or less, likely to contain a particular type of ore. But this classification can be done in other ways, without any 'millions of years' tag to it. For instance, calling a rock system 'Jurassic' can be done based on the sorts of fossils generally buried in it, quite independent of the ages. For instance, where our firm is now mining, the sedimentary rocks labelled as 'Precambrian' are highly likely to contain iron ore. So that's where we look for it. But you could just as easily classify these as 'pre-Flood' or 'early Flood' deposits. They could be classified by their position relative to other sedimentary layers, and the types of fossils they do or don't contain. Such a classification would be just as useful to the mining industry, without any 'millions of years' attached."

I asked Jim whether his many colleagues who believed in, or even taught, billions of years would recognize their bias. He agreed that many would not, but that when faced with the possibility that they might have been misled by such bias into believing something false, it was natural for many to become quite defensive, even emotional. He said, "If you think your whole life's work has been based on a lie, it naturally causes a reaction. The difficulty is to get them to realize that it's not that tied up with their work at all. Some 99 percent of our work as geologists has nothing to do with the millions-of-years belief at all. But this minor part has a major emotional impact, it seems." That may be why some of his colleagues have reacted strongly at first about his belief in Genesis creation.

"One of them was really upset when he found out," said Jim. "He said 'Come on, Jim, you don't really believe that rubbish, do you?' I think he was upset because he respects me. I like him, he's a

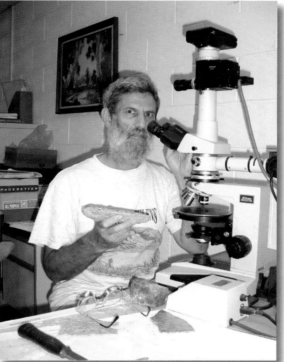

great guy. He made a bit of a scene and went home in a bit of a huff, but he has subsequently been very pleasant to me. He handed me a paper recently giving evidence for a younger Pilbara sequence than originally thought (still millions of years, of course) and said, 'You'd better read this, I suppose it is your sort of stuff.' "

Rocks don't speak for themselves

This brought to mind the whole issue of the way in which science interprets the past, through the filter of fallible and changing hypotheses and frameworks. Jim said, "When we geologists try to interpret what happened to form a particular set of rocks, it is not some hard

science, like testing the laws of gravity. It involves deduction, speculation, all sorts of fallible human opinions. The point is that the facts in the rocks don't just 'speak for themselves.' "

Jim said that there were several instances, relating to ore deposits with which he was familiar, where dogmas about how they formed, once strongly held, had changed completely. In the absence of being able to examine or repeat the past in the same way that experimental science functions, theories often competed on the basis of strong personalities and vehement arguments. He said, "I recall one time there were even fists involved at one conference. That is not to put down the competence or general integrity of geologists, just to make the point that interpreting the past is ultimately a fallible human exercise. Reconstructions based on all sorts of uncertainties are often presented as 'fact' when, if we're honest, they can't be presented that way."

Even though I already knew where he stood, I was left feeling encouraged. I know that Jim (like all of us at AiG) wants people everywhere to make a stand for the truth of God's Word, the Bible, and its good news of salvation for "whosoever will" cast themselves upon God's mercy through faith in Jesus Christ.

References and notes

1. Now somewhat outdated in its geological sections, this 1961 book has had the most powerful impact of any in triggering the 20th-century creation movement.

2. Australasian idiom for "lots."

"He Made the STARS Also . . ." GENESIS 1:1

Carl Wieland and
Jonathan Sarfati
interview Danny Faulkner

He determines the number of the stars and calls them each by name. Ps. 147:4

CW/JS: Dr. Faulkner, how did you get interested in astronomy?

DF: Well, I can honestly say there hasn't been a time in my life when I've not been interested in astronomy. I recall being three or four years old, looking up at the sky, being amazed at what was up there.

Many people have this image of an astronomer, sitting there each night staring into a telescope.

There really aren't any who spend all of their time looking through telescopes. The few research astronomers who do spend a good deal of time — they have to analyze the data they collect, write it up, plan future observations. So even the "full-time researchers" probably only spend about two months of the year actually observ-

Dr. Danny R. Faulkner has a B.S. (math), M.S. (physics), M.A. & Ph.D. (astronomy, Indiana University). He is associate professor at the University of South Carolina — Lancaster, where he teaches physics and astronomy. He has published about two dozen papers in various astronomy and astrophysics journals.

ing. Most astronomers, like myself, have an academic job teaching in a university or other related jobs and we do research when we can. Usually I get in 7 to 15 nights a year at a local observatory and a few more when travelling elsewhere.

How did you become a Christian?

I had a conversion at age six. My father was a minister of a small church and just as I can't remember not being interested in astronomy, I can't remember not going to church.

Some teach that the "big-bang" theory of how the universe evolved is such an obvious fact that we should accept it as if it had been written in the "67th book of the Bible."

That's absolute rubbish. I'm really concerned with people who put that much faith in the "big bang." It is the overwhelmingly dominant model, and they've had a few impressive predictions, like

the background radiation. But it has many problems — they keep changing the model to make it fit the data we have. As a Christian, my biggest concern is that it doesn't agree at all with the Genesis account of how the world came to be, and my big concern is that when you make that the fingerprint of God, as it were, then when the "big bang" is discarded, what does that do to Christianity?

Genesis teaches that the earth was created first and then the sun, moon, and the stars were created three days later. Is there any observation in your field of astronomy which would disprove this, or make it difficult to believe?

No. Most astronomers as well as geologists argue that the universe is aged 20 billion years, and the earth "scarcely" 4.5 billion years old. All that's really built upon a lot of indirect evidence and arguments — evidence that could very easily be interpreted other ways, and there are some other astronomical suggestions that the solar system and the earth and the rest of the universe are not really that old at all.

Can you give us some of these?

First, comets disintegrate too rapidly to have been in their present orbits for all those billions of years. So evolutionists theorize about a shell of comets, an "Oort cloud" too far out to see, to act as a way to "restock" the inner solar system with comets every so often.

However, there's no scientific reason to believe that there really is an Oort cloud. The so-called Kuiper belt, closer in, has been put forward as a theoretical source of shorter period comets. However, even if there are comets in this region, it doesn't solve the problem for the evolutionists, because the Oort cloud would still be needed to resupply the Kuiper belt after a while.

Then there is the moon. Due to tidal friction, this is slowly spiralling away from the earth, which is slowing down its rotation. If you calculate back a billion and a half years, the moon would have been in direct contact with the earth. So that is a very strong indicator that the moon can't be even a third as old as the claimed 4.5 billion years, and it is probably vastly less than that.

Also, theory suggests we should find plenty of, say, million-year-old supernova remnants, but we don't find any — though there are many that

are thousands of years old. And that is a very startling result if you really believe in a universe that's millions of years old.

How old do you think the universe is?

Probably six to eight thousand years.

Have you ever doubted what the Bible teaches about recent six-day creation?

Not seriously. I may have gone through a brief period when I was in high school or so, due to encountering people who were into theistic evolution, but then I got a copy of one of Henry Morris's early books. Then I learned more and more about other scientists who believed in a recent creation.

Why is it important to believe in this?

Well, we have a very clear indication from Scripture that the creation really took place in six ordinary days. And if you think it didn't, then you are going to have to ask the question, "How

do you *know* that it didn't happen that way?" Good biblical exegesis will simply not allow for a much greater length of time. And once you decide you are going to let "science" dictate how you are going to interpret Scripture, then there is no end to it. I recently read that former U.S. President Jimmy Carter was quoted as saying that he believes in the virgin birth, but he doesn't believe that the world was created in six days. I think if asked why not, he would say, well, because of overwhelming scientific evidence. And I think I would reply to that, the overwhelming scientific evidence is that a virgin birth is not possible. So be consistent on this point; one's a miracle, so is the other. If you don't believe in recent six-day creation, then it opens the door to serious doubts about the virgin birth, about the Resurrection; those would also be scientific "impossibles."

What about the argument that the universe must be old, because light would take millions of years to get here from distant stars?

That has long been the biggest challenge for creationists. There have been several suggested answers — one from Australia around 13 years ago was Setterfield's possible drop in the speed of light. When I first encountered that, I thought it was a pretty good idea, but there are a lot of consequences of that and I don't any more think it is the answer. Perhaps the most common idea is that God created the light in transit.

I have a real problem with that one. For example, when a distant supernova explodes, there is all sorts of detailed information in the light — the speed of expansion, what isotopes are involved, even sometimes a reflected light echo from nearby gas. Yet if the light was created "on its way," all this is phony information — nothing like it ever occurred. This reminds me of a fellow named Gosse who was saying over 100 years ago that God created fossils inside the earth ready-made. I think this "light created on its way" idea is a first cousin of Gosse's notion.

So what idea do you like?

I got really excited with the cosmology which Russ Humphreys presented a few years ago in Pittsburgh. It's the first serious attempt that young-world creationists have offered as an alternative for, first of all, the universe itself — cosmology — and second, a very detailed explanation for the distant starlight issue.[1] I think that's very impressive, and even if it turns out that Russell's not right, he's certainly leading the way in that kind of work.

What about stars claimed to be forming today?

Stars supposedly condensed out of vast clouds of gas, and it has long been recognized that the clouds don't spontaneously collapse and form stars, they need to be pushed somehow to be started. There have been a number of suggestions to get the process started, and almost all of them require having stars to start with. This is the old chicken and egg problem; it can't account for the origin of stars in the first place.

Stars are not very complex, and so-called "stellar evolution" (though I don't necessarily accept all of it) is a different critter from biological evolution. So I don't have a problem with the idea that a cloud of gas, created initially by God in a special unstable condition, or compressed by a shock wave from a nearby exploding star, might collapse under its own gravity and start to heat up to form a new star.

The Psalmist writes that the heavens declare the glory of God. What do you see as the best evidence for that?

I think the universe is a mighty beautiful place — I view God as the supreme artist. Then we see that there are a lot of incredible and unique things about the earth which make life possible. For example, as far as we know, liquid water only exists on the earth. We see water in vapor form in the atmospheres of several planets, in stars, and the material between them. We've identified water in solid form — on Mars, on asteroids and comets, possibly even on Mercury. But the only place we know for *sure*[2] that there is *liquid* water, one of the essential ingredients for life to exist, is on earth. Even if it were proven elsewhere, liquid water would still be an amazingly rare and precious commodity that the earth has in abundance.

References and notes

1. See Dr. Humphreys's popular book *Starlight and Time* (available from Master Books) for a lay and technical explanation of this model.

2. Note that there is now doubt about the claim of ice in moon craters (*New Scientist,* June 14, 1997, p.13). Dr. Faulkner said to us after the interview that the alleged evidence for subsurface liquid water on Europa, one of Jupiter's moons, is much more speculative and indirect than most think.

Danny Faulkner points out some of the breathtaking wonders of the night sky to his wife Lynette and son Seth. Even without a professional astronomer in the family, we can all enjoy the awe-inspiring beauty of God's heavens.

Don Batten and Jonathan Sarfati interview husband and wife *Dr. Stephen Grocott* and *Dr. Dianne Grocott*. Stephen is a leading international research scientist in industrial chemistry, currently with a major firm in Queensland, Australia. Dianne is a qualified medical practitioner and psychiatrist. They have spoken on several occasions for the *Answers in Genesis* ministry.

Interviewing two people at once was a new one for us, but it helped to have known Stephen and Dianne for some time. They shared how they each converted to Christ in their early thirties.

The Creation Couple

Whether challenging

secularists on creation

or abortion, this

dynamic duo packs

a powerful punch

Dianne: I was brought up in the church. I went to an Anglican girls' school, where I sang hymns to the Creator at assembly, and learned about evolution in the science lab, so at 15 I thought, "God is irrelevant; I'll have to look after myself." That ended any sort of Christian thing for me for a long time.

To have some purpose in life I studied medicine — to help people. Then I trained in psychiatry because there people were looked at as more of a whole person.

But psychiatry didn't have the answers either. We were taught "the truth" according to Freud, Jung, the behaviorists, and so on. But they contradicted each other. You picked one that you liked and believed that as "truth," but it did not solve people's real problems.

People would confess to us bad things they had done, and then we'd let them decide whether it was all right to continue doing them. I realized that I was like a priest, and it scared me. I tried all sorts of spiritual disciplines,

but didn't find the truth until some Christian friends invited us to a meeting. I responded to an invitation to follow Christ.

Stephen: I grew up believing that we came from the apes. I didn't have a Christian upbringing, but when I was about 15 I went to a Baptist youth group for about a year, primarily to play table tennis. I remember thinking, *I would really like to believe what these people believe, but I can't. That's just not the way the world is.*

By my early thirties I had had fantastic "success": a high-paid job, world travel, a lovely wife, but no peace; I was completely empty and without purpose.

When Dianne gave herself to the Lord, I thought it was just another thing which would pass, like Buddhism and other "isms" she had looked into. The pastor visited us to go through a tract with Dianne. I was eating, uninterested. He came to a page with man on one side of a chasm and God on the other, with the Cross as the bridge — Jesus. He was reading how man has his struggles, strife, pain, etc. and I thought, *That's life, big deal.* And then he said that in God there is peace. Bang! The Holy Spirit "grabbed" me. But I still had a question about evolution/creation. The pastor said, "The Bible says creation, so that's the way it is." So I just believed that, but wondered what my friends would say. So to

The Grocott family — Stephen, Patrick (6 weeks old), Rebekah (4), Dianne and Jeremy (7).

equip myself, I read voraciously. The materials from *Answers in Genesis* were just fantastic. For me, creation/evolution was not the key

> *". . . science is always changing and you would be constantly reinterpreting your reinterpretations of the Bible!"*

in coming to the Lord, but it has been *so* important in strengthening my faith since. Without that I would be just blown around.

We asked whether acceptance of six-day creation was important.

Stephen: As a scientist, I try to think logically — I just couldn't consider having a Bible where

some of it was true and some not — you believe the whole thing. I never tried to believe the days were long periods of time, or anything like that. It was just all or nothing. Some people say that we should leave aside the meaning of the days, that it is a stumbling block, but the true stumbling block is compromising God's Word.

Becoming a Christian, knowing that the whole Bible is true and God is the Creator — suddenly the whole picture made sense. The logic, and the watertight internal consistency of the Bible, and its consistency with what we see in the world, really impressed me. That's undermined by long-age beliefs.

We discussed the supposed conflict between "science" and the Bible.

Stephen: Though I'd been working as a scientist for ten years, I really only learned what science

A Handy Argument Against Evolution

For his Ph.D., Dr. Stephen Grocott worked on optically active compounds (these can exist in mirror-image forms of each other, like right and left hands). Life depends on having only pure forms of these (only one "hand"). But if life began in a chemical primordial soup, there was no means of supplying the necessary "single-handed" compounds. When Stephen synthesized optically active compounds, he always had to start with an optically active substance that was ultimately derived from a living source. With a bit of warming, his optically pure solution would decay back to a 50:50 mixture of right- and left-handed forms. He says:

"Even if there were some source of optical activity in a primordial 'soup,' it would quickly disappear anyway. The recent idea of polarized light from a nearby galaxy doesn't help. They talk of it possibly causing a slight imbalance, say 51 percent right-handed and 49 percent left-handed. But in time that will decay anyway, and you need 100 percent pure, not just a slight excess.

"I enjoy seeing the mental gymnastics of people trying to explain the origin of life. Most researchers in the area are honest enough to say they haven't got the faintest idea how life began from non-life. The mind boggles at the complexity of the simplest single-celled organism — and the more we learn, the more complex it looks."

was through *Answers in Genesis*. Some of the things people call "science" are really outside the realms of science; they're not observable, testable, repeatable. The areas of conflict are beliefs about the past, not open to experimental testing. Take radioactive dating. You can measure decay rates and isotope ratios today, but you can't extrapolate back to some time in the past when you couldn't measure it.

I've been asked if disbelieving evolution hampers my research. It doesn't, because I work in real, experimental science. But belief in creation gave me an appreciation for the beauty of what I was researching.

A proper scientific hypothesis needs only one contrary observation to prove it wrong. With evolution, you do not observe the predicted accumulation of information — you see a loss of information. And you do not see the millions of transitional forms there should be. So, if evolution was a scientific concept, it's been falsified.

So why do scientists believe in evolution? The same reason anyone believes in it — because everyone else, including scientists, seems to, and it's what you are taught. Also, for a non-Christian, the alternative (creation) can be unpalatable.

We inquired about those who say that we should re-interpret the Bible to fit in with "science."

Stephen: That shows a lack of understanding of science. In science you make observations, you try to come up with a hypothesis, an explanation that works, and you publish it. But a later experiment may show the hypothesis is wrong, and so you change it. So science is always changing and you would be constantly reinterpreting your reinterpretations of the Bible!'

Dianne's work changed radically, as she shares:

It was amazing. The hardest thing was realizing that I now had the truth, that God had the answers to people's problems, but I didn't know how it fit with my work. In spite of secular psychiatrists gradually recognizing a spiritual component to people's lives, they basically don't deal with that. They might send someone to, say, a meditation course, but the "spirituality" is very much "New Age" — i.e., "God" *is* "everything," rather than being the Creator who *made* everything.

Doing a course in Christian counselling made me even more unsettled, because I now had some tools that I could not use where I was working, in the public service.

I then had children and was out of psychiatry for a while. That was good, because I had been very evolutionized. Before I could work as a Christian psychiatrist I had to unlearn a lot of evolutionary thinking.

Later, I went into private practice with a group of Christians. It's great having the freedom to address spiritual issues, as well as biological, social, and psychological ones as appropriate. When Christians seek help with unresolved spiritual issues, I am free to help. People know they are coming to a Christian counseling center, so with people who know nothing of God but are receptive I can sow seeds or at least pray for them.

Is the "boom industry" of counselling a symptom of a society that has turned its back on God?

Dianne: Absolutely. Many people are looking for answers, but in the wrong places. True life is not found in drugs, addictive behaviors, the pursuit of possessions, or achievement. These contribute to a lot of psychological distress for which people seek help. Secular counseling and medication are often helpful but they don't fix the deep down problems of people who don't know God — who don't have a purpose for living. You have to be reunited with your Creator for that. Our society, our schools, the media, are telling us we're insignificant specks in a meaningless universe, but God says He sent His Son to die for us.

Stephen's work in industry has made him a target for the radical Green movement.

Stephen: I see in it a worship of the creation — it's the God-in-everything idea again — not the Creator. God makes it clear that He wants us to care for His creation, to be stewards of it. That means we are not to abuse the resources, but to use them sensibly, and for His glory. But in "Green" thinking, man is not the pinnacle of God's creation; he is just another evolving animal. When you see how they value animals over human life, it's pretty scary.

Dianne sees the impact of "we are just animals" in her involvement in the Right-to-Life movement.

Dianne: If we're just evolved animals, why not have an abortion if the lady feels like it? Most people don't really understand how abortion can affect not only the baby, but also the mother and the father, long-term. If you kill your child, you can't go back to the time before the pregnancy. You are now the mother (or father) of a dead child. Even non-Christians feel grief, guilt, and loss of self-respect. I've seen people who have felt so bad after abortions, they've gone into promiscuity, drug abuse, or depression. But I've also seen the Lord forgive, heal, and restore lives damaged by abortion.

In medical school, Dianne was taught the fraudulent "embryonic recapitulation" theory, in which human embryos were supposed to go through a fish stage, then an amphibian stage, etc.

Dianne: This idea has been used to persuade women that abortion is not destroying a human. But those in the abortion industry know they are dealing with live children who become dead children. That's why abortion clinics do not show the pregnant woman the ultrasound of the baby.

I have met women who were told after abortions, "Here is your blob of tissue," but it was the afterbirth; the broken parts of the baby went into another bucket. They were lied to, but if we all just evolved, and the Bible isn't true, why should an abortionist worry about God's commandments against lying — or murder?

Many think oil takes millions of years to form. But Stephen has been researching the rapid formation of oil from rock.

Stephen: You can heat the organic precursor to oil, kerogen (a polymer derived from plants and algae, and found in certain rocks), in the absence of oxygen and get oil in seconds. And even at temperatures less than 300°C, this will happen by "hydrous pyrolysis," in the presence of certain clay minerals, which are as common as muck. You get such conditions beneath the earth. I am not saying it takes seconds to form kerogen, then oil, but it certainly does not need millions of years — under the right conditions it only takes months, decades, or hundreds of years.

Both Stephen and Dianne see lots of evidence for a Creator in their fields.

Stephen: I see the beauty of the way that molecules go together, the systematic nature of chemical structures, and the laws that govern their formation and arrangement. I look at that and I say, "Man, this is complex, but it fits together by all these really neat rules. Where do they come from?"

The chemistry of life is scarily complex. That people can even contemplate it making itself staggers me. Speaking to colleagues about it, they often get themselves into a logical corner, and then it gets down to the bottom line — a spiritual issue. It is *willful unbelief.*

Dianne: I see "design" in the way human beings are meant to relate to God and to each other. I see people who are angry, sad, guilty, perturbed, and distressed in many different ways. When people get right with God a lot of problems often improve. Over time, their relationships with others improve, and as their symptoms improve they may not need as much, or any, medication. Some psy-

chiatric illnesses have a biological basis (genetic mutations have been accumulating since the Fall). Getting right with God allows people to cope better with illness and other challenges. There is increasing research showing that people with faith enjoy better mental health and relationships. Evolution-based attitudes ("the strong wipe out the weak" — opposite to what God has designed) favor violence, exploitation, and abuse, which do not lead to peace and joy.

Stephen and Dianne found that their marriage took on new meaning and stability when they both submitted to Christ:

Dianne: As an evolutionist, I believed that marriage was basically getting what you need from the other person, so you have to enter into a sort of contract. You're constantly in a state of tension, trying to make sure that you get as much as you need without losing too much. Christian marriage is not like this. It is God helping two people be together and be one, and when you get to the point where God meets your needs, you can be free to serve each other.

To each I would say, "Look to God to meet all your needs, and be prepared to lay down your life for your spouse, to give all on the mission field of his or her life, and God will supply your needs." Doing that, marriages start to really change. And the closer couples get to God, the closer they get to each other. I have seen that in the counseling room and in my marriage.

Stephen: Before we became Christians, we might have had another couple of years left and then it would've been all over. As Christians now, we say that God has written the rulebook about marriage, and about everything else, in His Word. Sometimes you don't want to do what He says, but you do it and when you see the results you have to say, "Wow!"

Flying High

Photo by Ken Ham

Dr. Andy McIntosh is a full professor of thermo-dynamics (holder of the chair) at Leeds University, U.K. with a background in aerodynamics. He was interviewed in Melbourne, Australia, by Chris Field.

Thermodynamics

Dr. Andy McIntosh

* Photo by Robert Doolan

CF: Dr. McIntosh, what does your work involve?

AM: Anything which works and uses energy has to have power, so power generation is a very important matter. Whether it's coal or nuclear energy, we need to know how to use it carefully, efficiently, and without danger. Now, it's the "without danger" bit where I come in. I've done a lot of studies in explosions and hazards of various kinds.

Such as?

Like if coal is transported in ships, and is left too long with air able to get at it, then because there isn't enough room to get rid of the heat, the coal gradually heats up and you can have a fire at sea. It involves some interesting problems.

But you're visiting Australia to talk to other scientific people about applied mathematics, aren't you?

I enjoy playing around with the equations, but I really like getting my feet down to the ground and talking with real people about real problems. Leeds University is known all over the world for its interest in practical problems in the energy scene.

I'm part of a Centre of Combustion there which straddles three departments — physical chemistry, mechanical engineering, and fuel and energy, and it's my job to make sure that center works. We have research seminars, and I track through students doing a year's master of science degree, for example.

I understand that you're dubious about evolution?

I guess that's an understatement, Chris. I'm not saying that the studies of scientists who work on evolution theory are all wrong. It's just that they're starting with certain assumptions, and that's what needs to be exposed.

Can you give an example of a misleading assumption?

One of their basic premises is that you cannot have design, it's ruled out of court. Now to my mind it is crazy to dismiss something without even letting it be a possible option. Many aspects of nature show that creatures have been designed.

What's your favorite example?

Creatures which fly. I got here to Australia on a great big jumbo jet. I watched the careful maneuvering as it came down to land, as the great big flaps came out at the back, increasing the size of the wing to get more lift so as to fly at a much slower speed. I was struck by all the design that went into that wing in order to make sure it worked. Now, are we to say that the birds which come to land every day weren't designed? I have seen a photo in a book of an aircraft landing at Hong Kong, and underneath it is a falcon landing at the same time. Now as you look at birds and planes together (see photo p. 74), are you going to say that one is designed and the other isn't? I would find that scientifically preposterous.

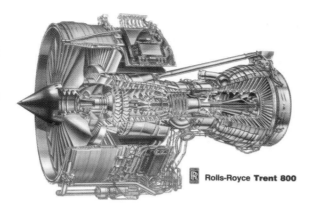

It takes enormous intelligent effort to design just the engine for a flying plane; how much more intelligence was required to design the first living, flying birds?

Rolls-Royce Trent 800

We know that in order for modern flight to take place, countless thousands of man-hours and much high technology had to go into the design process.

Indeed — I would take issue with people like [atheistic Oxford professor] Richard Dawkins, with his view that flight somehow came about by chance, just because some creature took a jump, then mutation added bits to its structure, so it could jump farther, and so on. It just doesn't fit. It's obvious that these creatures have not come about by chance and selection, but have in fact been designed.

What does the fossil record show about this?

You find that those creatures which are flying now and are also fossilized in the rocks were essentially the same then as they are now. There is no sign at all of any gradual evolutionary change. Butterflies are exactly the same in the fossil record. And yet it's claimed (I don't accept it at all) that they are hundreds of millions of years old. When it comes to birds, they're essentially, structure-wise, the same. And bats are exactly the same in the fossil record as they are today.

Why the particular interest in flight?

Well, I am originally an aerodynamicist — my Ph.D. was in an aerodynamics department. Bird flight in particular is remarkable; consider feathers. If you look at a feather under a microscope, you see the main stem, with barbs coming out to the left and right, and from these you have left- and right-handed barbules. Now the interesting bit is that the left-handed ones have hooks, and the right-handed ones have ridges.

That's so the feathers lock together. . . .

That's right. The feather is made such that if you bend it, everything bends with it, and yet it's a very light structure. So the hooks catch the ridges and they slide over the ridges — it's a mechanical engineer's dream to have such useful, lightweight engineering. But if you have a sliding joint, you need lubrication. To do this the bird twists its neck around 180 degrees and dips its beak into a tiny oil gland right down at the back of its spine. It then preens itself, wiping this oil all over its feathers, so that they join together nicely, and these sliding joints are oiled. That's a marvellous bit of engineering. So is the fact that

All flesh is not the same: Men have one kind of flesh, animals have another, birds another and fish another.
– 1 Corinthians 15:39

the whole of Western culture. Now we are very wrong to throw it overboard. Thomas Huxley ["Darwin's bulldog" — Ed.] knew full well last century that the way to undermine Christianity was to attack Genesis. Of course, he was very successful in getting his own thinking to usurp the authority of the Bible, and we are now reaping the results.

What about the fossils — don't they suggest a long time period?

In fact, I find it very difficult to believe that fossils formed slowly. The alternative way of looking at the rocks is to believe what the Bible tells us about a massive catastrophic Flood, and there is a lot of evidence to support that view. For instance, we have jellyfish as fossils (see photo at top of page 75). Now you've got to bury a jellyfish quickly in order to

birds, unlike us, have hollow bones. To be strong enough, particularly in the bigger birds, these lightweight bones often have cross-members. In aircraft we call the design "Warren's truss," but we copied it from birds in the first place.

So the incredible design in living things is a major objection to evolution?

Absolutely. I would say, frankly, that that's the major *scientific* reason why I could not for a moment hold to evolution. Design is shouting at me everywhere.

What about Andy McIntosh, the Christian?

Genesis gives us the basis for the only correct way to look at the world, because God has told us how everything came to be. We are not at liberty, as Christians, to think that there is a "both . . . and" situation here.

Evolution and long ages is completely contrary to what the Bible says.

That would sound radical to some.

Maybe, but it wasn't radical a hundred years back. Genesis creation is in fact what our society was based upon,

A plane and a bird (inset)—both exhibit design, the bird being far more complex.

Photo of plane by Ken Ham

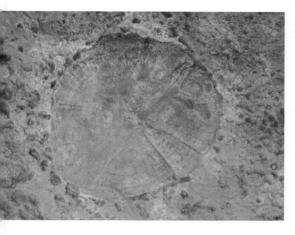

A photo of a jellyfish fossil from the Ediacara region of South Australia. For a fragile creature to leave such an impression indicates rapid burial and hardening of the sediment. Millions of similar soft-bodied creatures have left impressions in this vast area of sandstone, indicating a massive catastrophe.

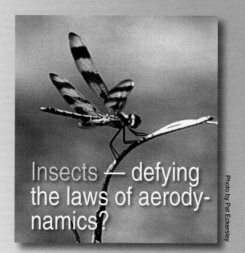

Photo by Pat Eckersley

Insects — defying the laws of aerodynamics?

leave its impression behind. It just won't last long enough to be slowly covered.

So you believe in a world created about 6,000 years ago, cursed on account of sin, then devastated by Noah's flood.

Absolutely. There's nothing in real science (if you take all the assumptions into account) to contradict that view.

What would you say, as a physical scientist, about radiometric dating?

Something's wrong with the radioactive dating method. They've dated New Zealand volcanic lava which we know flowed last century and the result says it hardened millions of years ago. The same occurred with the lava dome that's formed at Mt. St. Helens since the 1980 eruption. We can't trust the methods — the assumptions behind them are clearly shaky. It's a shame that some Christians today are being pressurized into doubting the Word of God, which is infallible, because of these fallible methods.

Dr. McIntosh — thank you.

Photo by David Menton

A feather under the microscope at two levels of magnification, showing the amazing intricacy of design. The interlocking hooks and barbules allow the feather to be "reset" by the bird's preening action.

It has often been said that, according to the laws of aerodynamics, insects shouldn't be able to fly. But of course they do — brilliantly. Actually, that only highlighted our ignorance of aerodynamics. Research over the past few years is revealing how insects do manage to fly in ways which put the achievements and maneuverability of our most advanced aircraft to shame.

Conventional analysis showed that insects were generating only about one-half to one-third of the lift needed to carry their weight. However, ingenious experiments have now shown unexpected patterns of vortex flow along the edges of insect wings.

These generate the extra lift needed because the vortex (a spiraling tube-like pattern of airflow like a mini-tornado) stays "stuck" to the leading edge of the wing for long enough.[1] At this point, no one knows how or why this particular vortex phenomenon occurs, but researchers have been able to see it in a robot model of a moth's wing inside a wind tunnel.

One reason why previous models failed to detect how insects could fly is that they used fixed wings. However, insect wings have a very complex motion, rotating and changing the camber. It required sophisticated programming to make the "robot insect" flap properly. This demonstrates how sophisticated the (created) design of actual insect flight must be.

References and notes

1. "On a Wing and a Vortex," *New Scientist* 156(2103): 24–27 (October 11, 1997).

An interview with creationism's "Mr. Ice Age" – weather scientist Michael Oard – by Carl Wieland

Tackling the

Michael J. Oard has a master's degree in atmospheric science from the University of Washington. Before retiring, he worked as a meteorologist/ weather forecaster for the (US) National Weather Service, and has published several papers in his field in widely recognized journals.

Big Freeze

When I first spoke with Michael (Mike) Oard, he jokingly "put down" the state where he lives as "home to the (maybe) Unabomber and a bunch of other interesting people."

Montana is in fact a beautiful part of the United States, one associated with rugged backwoodsmen and scenic wilderness. It is also a place where one can see a lot of evidence that large chunks of the world were once covered by huge glacial sheets. For example, Mike points out there are huge boulders which show signs of having been transported a long way from their original location. He says this was either from their being carried by an ice sheet, or dropped from an iceberg floating in one of the many lakes which were abundant near the ice sheet.

Although he does a lot of thinking and part-time research into other aspects of creationism, particularly in regard to the Flood, Mike (who has written quite a number of items for our associated *Creation Ex Nihilo Technical Journal*) is best known for his work on the biblical Ice Age. He has written a technical monograph on the subject, as well as *Life in the Great Ice Age*, a family book

coauthored with his wife, Beverly. This book really makes the subject "come alive" with its clever use of illustrated fiction, as Neanderthals and other post-Flood groups of humans interact with the harsh climate conditions.

Raised in a liberal church, Mike was taught that "there were errors in the Bible and all that sort of thing." However, when he read

Mike frequently contributes to AiG's peer-reviewed journal TJ *(formerly* Technical Journal*).*

it for himself, it "seemed reasonable." In spite of getting "a lot of religious education," it wasn't until a stint in the Navy that he thought seriously "about whether God existed, and if He existed, that's all that mattered."

Mike earnestly searched for evidence of whether God was real, and the Lord kept on bringing him back to creation. As time went on, he increasingly realized that "if you start messing with something that's reasonable, clearcut, and straightforward, which is God's Word, you get a lot of serious problems with all of Scripture." He believes that six-day creation is really important, because, he says, "If you start compromising that which seems to me very obvious in Scripture, you're opening yourself up to compromise in many other areas of the Bible, and that's what I think a lot of people do."

Mike says that he first began to think seriously about the mechanism for an ice age about 20 years ago, when he noticed that the evidence for the boundary of the North American ice sheet was right at the edge of where the present-day "permanent" winter snow accumulates. He says that "putting that together with ideas that other creationists have had over the years" was the key.

The important thing for any ice age theory, he says, is to find a way "to cool the summers, to stop ice from melting — in most areas that were once glaciated, the winters are already cold enough." One such cooling mechanism was readily available after the Flood, with much volcanic ash and gases still in the air from the breaking up of the crust which also liberated the "fountains of the great deep" described in Genesis. Such volcanic matter in the air would reflect much of the sun's heat back out to space.

However, just having cooler air is not enough. Mike points out that in Siberia today, there are very low tem-

Glacial ice

peratures, but it is so cold that there is not enough moisture in the air to maintain an ice sheet. To have an "ice" age, he says, you need a way to get lots of water out of the ocean up on to the land.

"After the Flood you would have both," says Mike. "The water that the Bible indicates came from under the ground during the Flood would have been very warm or hot. This water mixing with the pre-Flood ocean would result in a significantly warmer ocean, right after the Flood, than today. Warmer water means more evaporation. So you have more moisture in the air available for storms, generating snow and ice at middle and upper latitudes, close to the developing ice sheets. And

the ash and gases in the air is what gives the cooling of the summers." All this, he points out, would have been like a "loaded gun" at the end of the Flood. "There would have been no way to delay it; an ice age just had to start."

Evolutionists, says Mike, have a favored astronomical theory for the Ice Age which gives them a little cooling, but no way to get more moisture into the air (a *colder* world means less evaporation from the oceans).

Mike Oard's calculations show that a likely estimate for when the Ice Age reached its maximum would have been around 500 years after the Flood, with about another 200 years to melt. He warns that this is only a "ballpark" figure, which could vary by hundreds of years, "but that's still a short time for evolutionists."

What about the riddle of the frozen mammoths? Mike says he is sure that they were the result of post-Flood events, since most of them are found in the frozen so-called "muck" on top of Flood sediments, in cliffs which are actually river deltas, or on marine shorelines. "They're actually rather surficial, and although scientists estimate there are hundreds of thousands, or millions of mammoth skeletons in Siberia, there are only several dozen which have flesh on them, and this is mostly scraps. There are only a few fairly intact carcasses, like the Beresovka mammoth in the Leningrad museum. Some of these were found with stomach contents only partially digested."

Does this prove they were frozen extremely rapidly, as one frozen food company suggested? Mike replies, "The Beresovka mammoth was preserved largely by freezing, but it didn't have to be a supercold 'snap freeze.' A mammoth with some stomach contents was found in the Midwest of the United States, where the ground isn't frozen at all. So there may be other mechanisms at work."

Does this mean no evidence for catastrophe? "Oh, no," says Mike. "There is no doubt that there has been a permanent, rapid climate change in northern Siberia/Alaska. Today, the ground there, in which these mammoths are buried, is permanently frozen, so you couldn't push a mammoth into it today. The vegetation today is too sparse to support large herds of mammoths anyway. After the mammoths were buried in it, the ground had to become frozen fast enough to preserve the flesh which is found, and has stayed that way since."

Though he doesn't claim to have all the answers, Mike speculates that these creatures died at the very end of the post-Flood biblical Ice Age, when the vast sheets were melting, bringing in permanent climate change and also catastrophic flooding events when huge lakes burst through ice dams. "Believe it or not," he says, "summers would get warmer, but winters would get a lot colder, developing a permafrost." He says there is published evidence of a massive catastrophic burst of an ice dam in Siberia, on the scale of the Spokane Flood which carved the

channeled scablands of the northwest United States. As huge amounts of fresh water surged into the Arctic ocean, it would cause a drop of up to 30 degrees

Glacier at Prince William Sound, Alaska.

Celsius in around a week.

"It's hard to freeze saltwater, but when a mass of fresh water (which floats on top of the saltwater) pours into a region with sub-zero temperatures, you could freeze much of the Arctic ocean surface within days. The air above this sea ice is deprived of heat and moisture from the ocean. The snow that soon falls will reflect much of the sunlight back to space, cooling the air further.[1] As a result, there would be a tremendous cold front over the land which, with the added wind chill, could possibly explain the frozen mammoth carcasses."

Mike says that secular scientists have been deafeningly silent about his published work. The only exception was a vigorously anti-creationist geophysicist who, Mike says, "could only point to a few real small points he thought were mistakes, and I don't think they were — and he said there isn't all this volcanic dust in the sediments, but I went back and found out that there is, so he wasn't correct on that. And he hasn't said anything since." Mike Oard is convinced, as a scientist, that the Ice Age gives excellent evidence for the real history of the world given in the Bible.

References and notes

1. These effects, Mike explained, would overwhelm the much more modest amount of heat liberated as the fresh water froze.

It Doesn't Take a Rocket Scientist

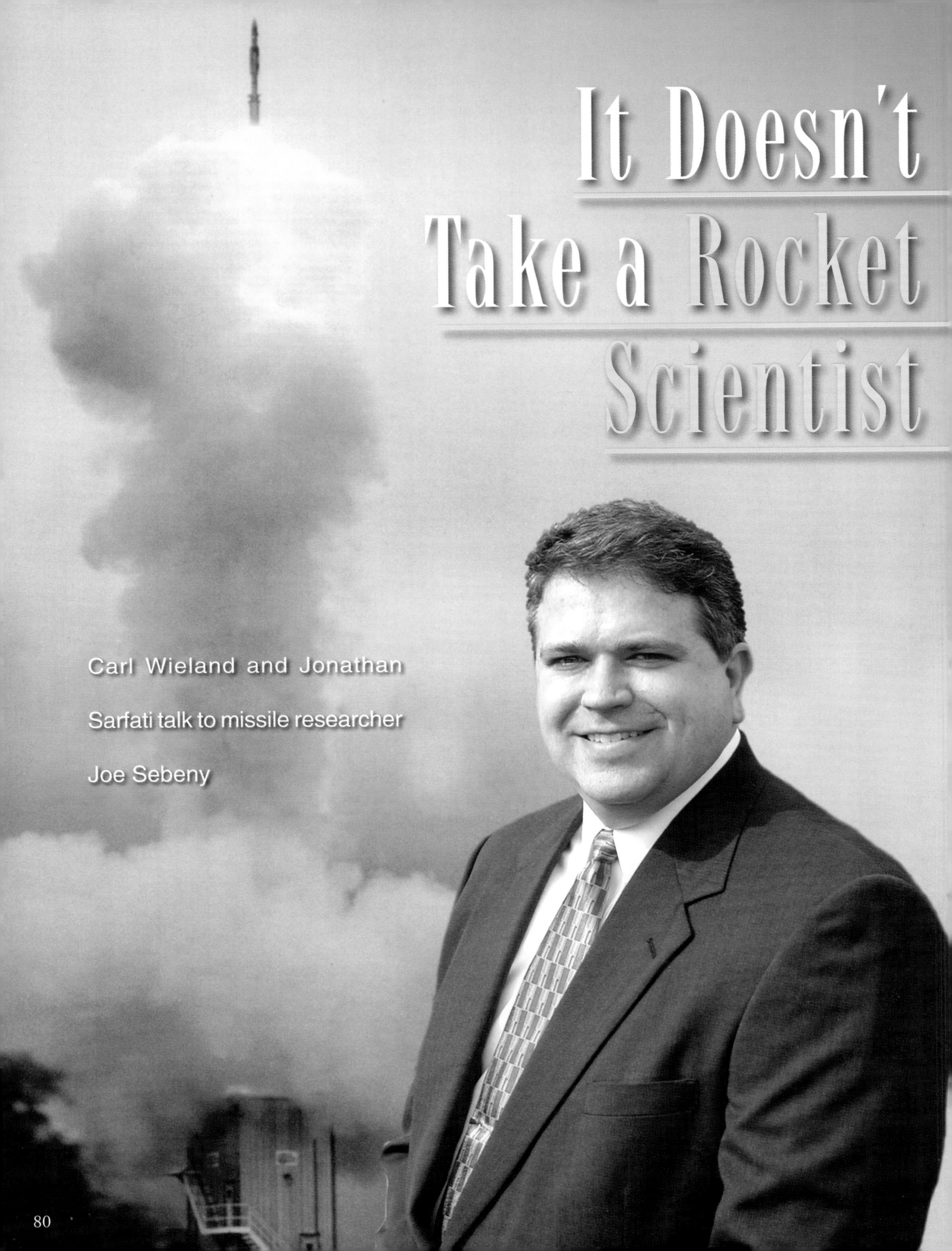

Carl Wieland and Jonathan

Sarfati talk to missile researcher

Joe Sebeny

Chatting with someone who designs rockets for a living and soundly rejects evolution makes it hard to resist this variation on a common quip: "It doesn't take a rocket scientist to figure out that something's wrong with evolution/long ages."

Joe Sebeny really *is* a rocket scientist. An aerospace engineer with over 20 years of experience in the defense industry, he works for Raytheon Company, the world's largest tactical missile producer, in Tucson, Arizona. Somewhat of a child science prodigy, Joe graduated from high school three years early with special honors. He earned two degrees from Massachusetts Institute of Technology, one in physics, the other in aeronautical/astronautical engineering, when barely 19. After this came a master's degree in electrical engineering from the University of New Hampshire.

The incredible design and complexity exhibited by living things is a major plank for Joe's firm rejection of evolution. He stresses that, as the leader of a project team, he is responsible for designing things that *work*. As he says, "I know how complex and difficult that is. We spend hundreds of millions of dollars and loads of intelligent man-hours making something work that is *nowhere near* as complex as a living thing — say, a bird. Yet the seeking sensors on our best missiles pale into insignificance next

to the incredible sensory abilities of the eyes of, say, the Peregrine falcon as it hunts. But people today, even many of my engineering colleagues who really should know better, are conditioned to switch off their brains and slip into the belief that these things are undesigned, that there is no ultimate, historical information source for all the incredible information in those living things."

Joe says that he believes in a young earth for both biblical and

> "If it were true that time makes all things possible, then indeed I could interpret the laws of thermodynamics anyway I wanted to, and it would be conceivable that energy from the sun could, given enough time, transform telephone poles into the most complex of flying machines. But it won't happen . . . ."

scientific reasons. "The best way to read any part of the Bible is straightforwardly, the way it was meant to be understood.

"I was raised in a Christian home," he went on, "and reading Genesis as a child, the meaning was very clear — what God did, how long He took, what order He did things in. Also, it told me that the original creation was very

good, before man's sin messed it up and death entered the world. Long-age thinking doesn't add up, as it has God calling millions of years of death and bloodshed 'very good.' "

We asked Joe how, as a person with solid credentials in physics, he responds to the claims that radiometric dating proves an old earth. He says, "Science tells me that it is absolutely impossible to age-date anything without knowing something about the history of what you are trying to date. You need to make a whole bunch of assumptions, but without someone to tell you to some extent what the history was, you have no idea whether your assumptions are correct or not."

So why do so many make the assumptions they do? Joe says, "Second Peter chapter 3 basically tells us that there are two important events in history that you mustn't ignore, but predicts that a time would come when people would willingly ignore them anyway. One is special creation, the other is the Flood. Any type of age calculation that doesn't take those two things into account is bound to come up with wrong answers."

Rockets being associated with space issues, we asked Joe for his views on reconciling a young world with stars that are huge distances away. He said that,

A wall of fire appears around this AE-GIS-ER (extended range) surface-to-air missile (SAM) being launched from a U.S. Navy cruiser. Joe was one of the lead engineers involved in the design and testing of this missile.
Photo courtesy of Raytheon Company.

(Right) Joe's family — Deann, Andrew, Nathan, and Joe.

scientifically, he feels drawn to the hypothesis put forward by Dr. Russell Humphreys in the layman's book (with technical appendices) *Starlight and Time*. (This model starts with different philosophical assumptions to the atheistic assumptions used in "big bang" thinking. Using the same equations, i.e., Einstein's general relativity, a different cosmology emerges. As a side effect, one sees how the experimentally demonstrated effect of gravitational time dilation means that light could traverse billions of light years while the whole universe is created in six normal-length days.)

"I've become somewhat of a fan of Humphreys, and think he is likely onto something here," says Joe, who adds that relativity was one of his favorite university subjects.

He has enjoyed watching "the debate" as Humphreys has been dealing with his long-age critics in our peer-reviewed science journal, *TJ*.

Flying telephone poles

Light-heartedly, Joe says, "I like to describe myself as someone who makes telephone poles fly. Our missiles have proportions not too dissimilar to telephone poles."

For by him all things were created: things in heaven and on earth, visible and invisible, whether thrones or powers or rulers or authorities; all things were created by him and for him.
– Colossians 1:16

More soberly, he recalls reading about a framed quote hung in a missile-making executive's office in the 1960s: "The technical axiom that nothing is impossible sinisterly conditions one to the pitfall corollary that nothing is ridiculous." Joe sees that as a great statement about evolutionism, especially if one were to add, after "nothing is impossible," the commonly heard phrase, "given enough time."

"If it were true that time makes all things possible," says Joe, "then indeed I could interpret the laws of thermodynamics any way I wanted to, and it would be conceivable that energy from the sun could, given enough time, transform telephone poles into the most complex of flying machines. But it won't happen, and the same laws make the evolution of a living thing from lifeless raw ingredients equally impossible, no matter how much time is imagined."

We asked Joe whether people ever said that it was inconsistent for him as a Christian to be involved in making weapons of destruction. He replied, "I haven't had that problem much. Just once in a while. I believe the Bible makes it *very* clear that we are allowed to defend ourselves."

Joe Sebeny loves handing out copies of *Creation* magazine widely. He has been involved in personal creation outreach for some years, often in close collaboration with AiG personnel. For instance, he often goes to home school conventions, taking along materials supplied from AiG's U.S. office.

He says, "The theme of my ministry is that the Bible and true science are in perfect harmony, but the church has, I think, been very lax in defending Scripture, especially the first few chapters of Genesis. The compromise with 'science' that has gone on for the last 150 years or so has done great harm."

Joe sees creation ministry as an extremely useful tool for showing people that there is a Creator, and says, "It also points them to the entire biblical flow of history which is focused around Jesus Christ, His death, burial, and Resurrection.

"That's why I'm looking forward to being able to hand out copies of this article when it's finished, hoping it will engage folks with the gospel message woven throughout your magazine."

EXPLODING
the Big Bang!

Gary Bates talks with creationist physicist/ cosmologist John Hartnett

Dr. John G. Hartnett received his Ph.D. in physics, with distinction, from the University of Western Australia, where he is currently a post-doctoral fellow. His current research interests include ultra-low-noise radar; ultra-high-stability microwave clocks based on pure sapphire resonators; tests of fundamental theories of physics, such as special and general relativity; and measurement of drift in fundamental constants and their cosmological implications. He has published more than 30 papers in refereed scientific journals and holds two patents.

How did our universe come to be? This is one of the "big" questions, and scientists who study the origin and history of the universe (cosmos) are called cosmologists. Nearly all modern cosmologists believe that everything was "kick-started" by a "big bang"[1] about 15 billion years ago, where the universe suddenly emerged from an extremely hot and dense state.[2]

But one dissenter from this ideology is Dr. John Hartnett — this makes him a "rare breed" of physicist. He is one of a relatively small number of Bible-believing creationists worldwide involved in cosmological research and thinking.

Facts versus their interpretation

When they view distant stars that are millions of light-years away from the earth, many people, including Christians, have trouble accepting the biblical account that God created the universe about 6,000 years ago. But believing the Bible right from the start is not a problem for John, which puts him at odds with his evolutionary counterparts.

Often they will accuse him of denying reality ("Look, we can see it — it's obvious"). But John explains that when looking at the universe, it's no different than looking at the fossil record. "It's the *interpretation* of the evidence," he says. "Sure, distant stars and galaxies might be millions of light-years away, but that doesn't mean that it took the light millions of years, by our standards, to get here. A light-year is a measurement of *distance*, not time. (It is the distance that light would travel in a year through a vacuum at its current speed of 186,000 mph [300,000 km/h], that is, 5,878,000,000,000 miles [9,461,000,000,000 km].) In other words, it's just an expression used to tell us how far away something is — not how long it took the light to get here."

John did not always believe in Genesis creation. He explains that he was interested in cosmology from a very young age, and mixed with those of similar interests. When John was 16, he and a friend co-authored a cosmology book that won a local science contest.

Big bang founded on unprovable assumptions

He says, "At that time, I would have described myself as an atheist, believing that the big bang had all the answers, although there was actually very little in the way of specifics about this model. It was this that drove me into further investigation.

"Interestingly, most people think that the big bang has already been worked out, but they don't realize that there are differing versions of the big-bang model — and not everyone agrees. By inserting a few unprovable *assumptions* at your starting point, you can end up with virtually any model you like. The big bang *assumes* that the universe has no center or edge. Not only is this not proven, some recent research on red-shift patterns have badly damaged its credibility by indicating that our galaxy is at, or near, the center of the universe.[3]

"What I really find amusing," he says, "is the way people from various other fields of science often quote the big bang as if it's 'set in stone.' I don't wish to sound unkind, but because they are not experts in this field, many of them have no idea what the big bang is really all about and misunderstand it."

At present, John is assisting another creation scientist, Alex Williams, in compiling a book about the big bang from a creationist viewpoint. "We really want to show the scientific weaknesses in big-bang thinking, and that you can't fit it into the Bible," he says. Jokingly, he adds,

"We actually want to create a big bang of our own among the scientific establishment, and dispel the myth of this cherished icon of evolution."

Solving problems

John is not content simply to point out that a light-year is just a measure of distance, but tries to explain distant starlight from a biblical framework:

"The way I see it, the Bible is true and the stars were created on day 4. Yes, the universe is very large, but we also have a very great God. My personal view is that the explanation probably involves a certain amount of

Dr. John Hartnett

Sophisticated sapphires

Dr. John Hartnett showed us these man-made sapphires. Very pure crystals of aluminium oxide, they are used in the oscillator pumps his team develops for atomic clocks. He said, "The ones we are using in our clocks right now would cost around $20,000 each.

"We're currently working with the European Space Agency in developing technology to test their atomic clock that is going to be used on the International Space Station. The precision of clocks like those can be used to measure the effects that gravity has upon time, even on Earth."

miraculous activity during creation week.

"But I don't believe that we see any false information, like 'light created on its way.' This would mean that we would be seeing light from heavenly bodies that don't really exist; and even light that seems to indicate precise sequences of events predictable by the laws of physics, but which never actually happened. This, in effect, portrays God as a deceiver.

[This is very different from creating Adam as fully grown, looking like a 20 year old, say, although he was really only a few minutes old. Here there is no deception, because God has *told* us that he created Adam from the dust, therefore there *cannot* be any history of growing for 20 years from an infant. But God has also told us that the stars are real, and that they are signs, not just apparitions from light waves.[4]]

"There is every reason to anticipate a logical scientific explanation for all that we see. We don't deny that some research is still needed, as we don't yet know all the details — just as big-bang theorists face various problems and challenges."

In fact, John thinks this is an exciting time to be a Christian, particularly in the area of cosmology. He thinks that Dr. Russell Humphreys's book *Starlight and Time* has broken new ground for creation researchers in this area.

"What Humphreys has done," he says, "is show us another parameter of something that most people view as a constant, and that is *time* itself. Using Einstein's theory of general relativity, he has shown how time can vary depending on your position in space — it affects your viewpoint. Time is slowed by gravitational forces. A clock at sea level has been shown to run more slowly than one on top of a mountain, because the one at sea level is affected by more gravity. This is an effect known as *time dilation*, and has been experimentally demonstrated.

"Humphreys uses this to great effect in his model to deal with the distant starlight issue. His cosmology starts with the earth near the center originally, then the universe rapidly expanding in a 'white hole' or black hole running in reverse. At the beginning, gravity would slow earth 'clocks' far more than clocks farther away, especially at the edge of the universe. Therefore, 'billions of years' would be available (measured by clocks in those distant regions of space) for light to reach the earth, for stars to age, etc. — while less than one ordinary day is passing on earth (measured by earth clocks, on which biblical time is based)."

Cutting-edge research

John's current work is directly related to this field. As a research fellow with a prestigious secular university, he is part of a team that develops technology for very precise atomic clocks (see box about the special sapphire crystals, left). He explained that the clocks are so precise that they might only gain or lose about one second of time every 400 million years. "They tick so fast — about 10 billion times a second — that we can directly measure infinitesimal losses."

Cosmology and Christianity

John adds that since he became a Christian, he regards it as his "calling" to make cosmology more understandable for the average layperson. He says, "Modern ideas about the origin of the universe contain lots of complicated mathematical theories and formulas. Many people are duped into thinking that because two plus two equals four, the math of the big bang must be right. But in most cases, these formulas are not provable or testable — they remain completely theoretical, and the models they support are based on unprovable starting assumptions. Christians, in particular, should not be worried about this."

He is particularly critical of Dr. Hugh Ross's beliefs. That is, Ross "reinterprets" Scripture to claim the days of Genesis 1 were long ages, and tries to use the big bang as a proof of Christianity. He observes, "Hugh Ross is on very shaky ground — placing his faith in this model, particularly when the real big-bang leaders seem not to agree that the theory implies a Creator."

When I asked him about his history as a Christian, he reminisced about his young co-author friend. He recalls, "He got saved, and I became quite bitter toward him and other Christians. I used to go along to meetings and torment them. At one meeting I even tipped over a table full of books and stuff. I challenged them on evolution and origins, and they always avoided the subject. Looking back, though, I can remember having some doubts — a sort of belief in God, so if someone could have shown me some scientific basis like creation — in the Bible — I think it would have had a big impact on me."

Years went by, and John became a Christian during the third year of his undergraduate degree in physics. Meeting other Christians after that, one young man challenged him to read Genesis, saying, "Read the first part, and when you're finished, I'll come back and talk to you."

John says, "When I started reading it — it was like — wow, unbelievably amazing. Straight away it struck me that this could be completely consistent with the scientific evidence and the knowledge I had at that time. I was being converted into a creationist there and then."

In their enthusiasm, John (by now married) and his wife strayed for a while into a quasi-Christian cult. He remarks, "We thought we were serving God — we were so keen. But looking back, I don't think we ever really fitted in, and we now realize our mistake."

John realizes that the distant starlight issue is a major stumbling block to belief in the Bible; the controversy, he says, is aimed squarely at the Genesis account of creation, which is foundational to the gospel. He says, "I can understand it being an issue — it was a problem for me, too. But now I know that God did create it all, and when He says He did, I'm just eager to find out more about how. And, in the process, to help Christians give increasingly powerful answers to defend and share their faith."

References and notes

1. The term "big bang" was coined in derision by its illustrious opponent, Sir Fred Hoyle (1915–2001). See Hoyle's obituary, G. Demme and J. Sarfati, " 'Big-bang' Critic Dies," *TJ* 15(3):6–7, 2001; <www.answersingenesis.org/hoyle>.

2. However, although most people think of the big bang as an enormous explosion into space, leading big-bang proponents picture it as a rapid expansion of space itself, which carried the matter along with it.

3. R. Humphreys, "Our Galaxy Is the Centre of the Universe, 'Quantized' Redshifts Show," *TJ* 16(2):95–104, 2002.

4. See further discussion of why the "light in transit" is fallacious, and a plausible alternative explanation, D. Batten, editor, et al., *The Answers Book* (Green Forest, AR: Master Books, 1990).

Caving in to CREATION

Carl Wieland interviews Romanian geologist and world cave authority Dr. Emil Silvestru

(Background) The "Miniature Hall" in Pestera Humpleu, one of the most voluminous caves in Europe.

(Superimposed left) Dr. Emil Silvestru ascending on rope

Photo by D. Seliscan

Dr. Emil Silvestru

Emil Silvestru earned his Ph.D. from the Babes-Bolyai University, Transylvania, (where he has worked as an associate professor) in karst sedimentology. A world authority on the geology of caves, he has published 23 scientific papers, 6 abroad. He was till recently the head scientist at the world's first speleological institute ("speleology" is the study of caves).

Transylvania — to hollywood-soaked Western ears, the name of this Romanian province is likely to conjure up haunting images of swirling mists, vampire bats, and black-caped aristocrats with thick Bela Lugosi accents.

Actually, the Count Dracula of Bram Stoker's original novel prob-

ably derived from a real figure of Romanian history, the mid-15th century Prince Vlad. His father was Vlad Dracul,[1] so he was named Vlad Draculea ("son of Dracul"). Vlad junior earned his nickname,"Vlad the Impaler," by his habit of thrusting people alive onto sharpened stakes. He is said to have approached the problem of poverty by inviting all of his country's beggars and paupers to a free feast — then he burnt down the building with all of them in it.[2]

Sadly, Romania has yet to recover from a more recent bout of despotic evil, perpetrated by the notorious communist dictator Nicolae Ceausescu (1918–1989) prior to his overthrow in December 1989.

In a small Transylvanian town in 1954, Emil Silvestru was born into this shadowy post-war world

of repression, fear, and Communist secret police. From the age of 12, he began to be fascinated by the numerous caves and other karst[3] features in his region, which naturally led to the study of geology.

In 1979, after five years' study, he was awarded a master's degree[4] from the state university in Transylvania's capital, Cluj. During his student years, he had already begun to publish research papers on "karstology,"[5] an interdisciplinary study of the limestone region and its features (see photos page 90) which had captured his youthful attention.[6]

Following graduation, there was no point applying for a Ph.D. in geology. As Emil explains, until the 1989 revolution, "such things were decided by Ceausescu's semi-illiterate wife, Elena, who had decided against geology PhDs." So he spent the next

Photos by Emil Silvestru

(Above) The karst plateau where Emil worked for his Ph.D. Isolated firs (and the pond) mark dolines, funnel-shaped hollows typical of karst landforms.
(Left) This mini-canyon formed inside a karstic catchment depression in less than ten years. The sediments accumulated during periodic floods, when the "swallow hole's" capacity to pass water to the subterranean passage was overwhelmed.
(Below) One of the karst's most typical and spectacular features, called karren.

seven years in geological exploration in northern Romania. He gained experience in the geology of certain types of ore bodies, and discovered several deposits amounting to about a million tons of lead/zinc ore.

In this time, he says, "I continued my speleological [cave] investigations, discovering karst processes during the pneumatolytic[7] phase—a world first—and investigating many hydrothermal [hot water] caves as well."

In 1986, he began work at the Emil Racovitza Speleological Institute (the world's first, founded in 1920). He says, "My hobby had now become my jobby (job + hobby)."

His wife, Flory, a former athlete in Romania's national team, was a Baptist believer for many years before he was. He says, "This brought nothing but problems from the Communist regime. I had already begun to doubt the atheist dogma I had been taught. It was through my scientific work that I came to realize that the order, beauty, and sense of fine humor with which the world is built cannot possibly come from chaos and randomness—I was sure there was a Designer.

"And for a long time, that was enough for my inflated ego. I recall asking Flory, who was reading her Bible regularly, when she was going to finish 'that book.' I believe it was then that God began to work on me."

Secret meetings

Emil told me that even though watching Christian videos was illegal, it was very popular in a country groaning under Communist repression. When Zefirelli's film, *Jesus of Nazareth,* arrived in Romania on video, "secretly seeing it became a noble act of resistance to the regime," says Emil.

(Right) A bat colony in the cave Meziad, in which radioactive caesium (^{137}Cs) from Chernobyl was found in bat guano (droppings). Insects strongly concentrate radioactive fallout, and are eaten by bats.

(Middle) Impurities like iron oxide, magnesium, etc. in this stalagmite "forest" give it its colors. Dr. Silvestru says that according to ^{234}U / ^{230}Th dating, even though all these formed in a very small area and there seems no significant difference in the amount of drip water they receive today, some of the largest ones are "younger" than the smallest!

(Bottom) Emil knocks on a stalagmite to feel the vibrations to ensure it is well crystallized, a necessity for accepted radiometric "dating" of such structures.

Caves, Climate, and "Vast Ages"

Cave geology expert Dr. Emil Silvestru affirms that caves, which he says are post-Flood in origin, "have proved to be among the best recorders of past climates, with an exquisite record which sometimes allows high-resolution reconstructions."

His work also involves the $^{234}U/^{230}Th$ dating of speleothems (those features such as stalagmites which grow in caves). This method, which is said to be accurate to within a resolution of only one thousand years (one Ka), combined with the evidence of growth and lack of growth of speleothems during glacial and interglacial stages respectively is, he says, "one of the most revered assets of evolutionists today.

"The precise (dare I say, sometimes too precise!) correspondence of these with Quaternary stages simply mesmerizes geological professionals, who add to it such things as measurements of ancient magnetism, plus estimates of temperatures based on oxygen isotope ratios in speleothems, and so on. But there is one big problem

for someone like me, who has been going into caves for over 30 years; some of the speleothems, not thicker than 2–4 inches (5–10 cm) yielded 'ages' over 200,000 years. Given what is known about karst processes, this is virtually inconceivable.

"The dates are way too old. This would mean that the whole duration of the Quaternary needs to be greatly compressed. Presently, I regard my 'datings' as merely confirming that speleothem growth fluctuated with the colder and warmer stages of the last stage of the Ice Age, not as accurate datings in any absolute sense."

Dr. Silvestru explained to us that, even using

such "way too old" dating methods, no karstologists today would talk of "millions of years" to form cave structures — even by conventional dating methods, the oldest accepted "date" is about 600 *thousand* years. He has personal experimental knowledge of very rapid rates of growth — even lab vessels used to collect drip water have become covered in a thick layer of calcite rock within less than 10 years.

Growth rates for stalagmites of several centimeters per year have been measured. When one does the calculations using only one millimeter per year (a very slow rate), even assuming that growth totally stops during the very cold glacial periods, then, says Dr. Silvestru, "Even the tens of thousands of years assumed by evolutionists would mean we should see many more massive stalagmites than we actually find."

With so many meetings, there was a high risk of being caught by the secret police, "But God was in control," says Emil.

(Right) Flory Silvestru in Piatra Altarului, *an ordinary cave which was subsequently flooded, forming a pool, the water line of which is visible. The water, saturated with minerals, deposited a bright coat of crystals on the stalactites and walls.*
In the same cave:
(Far Right) Closeup of the crystals. (Below) Aragonite crystals. (Bottom right) Large crystals on the tip of one of the flooded stalactites. (This particular formation is known as "The Mace.")

"So I suddenly found myself going to remote places, sometimes isolated mountainous areas, often in poor peasants' homes, invited to help show the film. Sometimes up to three films in one night, *The Ten Commandments* and *Quo Vadis* in addition. We had no dubbing facilities, so I had to do the translation live, 47 times in all. After a while I was very familiar with the visuals, and I preferred facing the audience while translating. I couldn't help but notice the profound impact all this was having on people."

One night they had to travel to a secret location 29 miles (46 km) away. To minimize the chances of detection, Emil was taken there in one car, a Mercedes, and driven back in a different vehicle. He says it was "a mockery of a car — an old Romanian imitation of the Soviet *Gaz*. It took us five hours to get back. The outside temperature was -25 °C, so we were nearly frozen solid when we got back to my place."

Photo by D. Seliscan

One night, still not a Christian, he was booked to do the translating after he had spent four to five hours surveying in a mine which, he says, "was so full of gases that the open flame of a carbide lamp would not burn. It was a funny situation that night — my brain was so gassed I could hardly do the translation!"

With so many meetings, there was a high risk of being caught by the secret police. "But God was in control," says Emil. Just a month after he transferred from the area for a new job, one such clandestine showing was raided, and the video recorder and tapes he had been using were confiscated.

Miraculous escapes

God's providential care was also evident in what Emil calls "several opportunities to leave this world." In one, he was climbing a rock wall and fell, seemingly to his death. Yet even after a freefall of 65 feet (20 m), his fall was somehow stopped by his partner. In another, a huge rock falling 330 feet (100 m) was heading straight for him down a wall when it split into many pieces, none of which hit him or his colleagues.

Perhaps the most memorable was when Emil was wading through a narrow gorge. Massive boulders began falling from the top of the gorge, about 1,300 feet (400 m) directly above him. He says, "It is quite hypnotic to watch such an event from below. With the walls less than

Photos by Emil Silvestru

13 feet [4 m] apart, and me waist deep in water, there was very little chance I would survive. Yet, it happened."

Emil says, "All this made me understand that it was unfair to attribute my survival to my good reflexes. . . . As a scientist I had to accept that 'somebody upstairs' loved me. I started attending my wife's church regularly, and on one apparently ordinary evening in church, I accepted the Lord Jesus Christ as my Savior. The truth is that the long years of my wife's silent prayers for me were answered. Without her, I would still be wandering around on quicksand."

Christianity and science

"Once I became a Christian," Emil says, "I knew I had to 'tune up' my scientific knowledge with the Scriptures." He briefly tried to maintain belief in an old earth via a "gap" theory, but this was an unsatisfactory compromise for a thinker like himself. He says, "Although philosophically and ethically I accepted a literal Genesis from my conversion, at first I was unable to match it with my 'technical' side."

However, e-mail discussions with qualified creationist geologists, creationist books, *Creation* magazine and especially the *Creation Ex Nihilo Technical Journal* helped him realize what he calls "two essential things":

1. Given exceptional conditions (e.g., the Genesis flood), geological processes that take place extremely slowly today can be unimaginably accelerated.

2. The Genesis flood was global, not regional.

He says, "I had heard this before, but was unable to fully grasp its significance at first. It involved an incredible 'brainquake' in changing my scientific paradigm.

"These factors were immensely important in my conversion and my Christian life. I am now convinced of a six-day, literal, recent, Genesis creation. That doesn't mean that there are not still some unanswered problems, but researching such issues is what being a scientist is all about."

Glaciers underground?

One of the fascinating aspects of his research work involves glaciers that accumulate underground. Romania has eight caves with important perennial ice deposits, including the world's second largest (75,000 cubic metres of ice in over 1,000 layers). After Emil managed to attract the famous Laboratory of Glaciology in Grenoble, France, the first drilling in a subterranean glacier took place, producing 70 feet (21.3 m) of core. Emil's interests include the formation and development of ice in caves, and the study of ancient climates preserved in the ice and other karst sediments.

He says, "Our Romanian-French team identified the radioactive isotope cesium-137 from the Chernobyl accident in bat guano in a subterranean glacier. In another cave, we found such residues from the

Photo by D. Seliscan

(Bottom Right) A hall in the cave Ghetarul de la Scárisoara, *the world's second largest subterranean "glacier." The several hundred ice stalagmites are perennial, but change shape every year.*
(Above and page 88)The same cave, 80 m (260 feet) below ground. Note the asymmetry of the ice stalagmites in the photo on page 88. The curved sides stand toward the deeper, warmer parts, away from the colder zone around the ice block.
(Below) A core sample of compact ice between the drill bit and tubes, same cave.

1963 Nevada H-Bomb experiments, in sediments at the bottom of a 12 meter-deep lake — the first such discovery in karst aquifers." The H-Bomb findings were particularly surprising, since water can only get to the underground lake in question by seeping down through more than 800 feet (250 m) of limestone. This suggests that the rates involved are much faster than previously assumed, although Emil is commendably cautious, saying that more data is needed from other caves.

Dr. Silvestru says that in the Romanian karst, there is no real proof

of caves older than the Quaternary, which "greatly simplifies a creationist interpretation, since it is consistent with the Bible." He believes that the currently prominent creationist modeling of the post-Flood Ice Age[8] is an important tool in understanding the karst in a young-earth framework.

I asked whether he experienced any ridicule or persecution because of his strong stand on Genesis creation. He replied, "Not really, for two main reasons. First, after so many years of almost compulsory atheism/evolutionism, most people welcome biblical creationism as a breath of fresh air. Second, God has granted me a professional status that practically bars any attempt to ridicule my creationist convictions. During public meetings on creation, even when academics are present, there are questions, yes, even strong arguments, but never ridicule. But I do believe that if I were very outspoken within our rather closed scientific community, many would reject or avoid me."

Along with a few academics and others, Emil is involved in the embryonic national creationist movement, as well as in translation of creation books.[9] One of the two existing groups, founded two years ago, is named after N.C. Paulescu, a Romanian creationist scientist who discovered insulin. Emil says, "Unfortunately, his discovery was made in Romania where there was little exposure to media. So a year later, two Canadians were credited with the discovery."[10]

Emil told me he would love to be able to devote himself to full-time creationist research, looking at such things as how a world with higher CO_2 (which may well have been the case before the Flood, and just after, before the earth was revegetated) might affect limestone deposition and rates of karst formation — in addition to refining his scientific critique of radiometric karst dating methods.

So it was a real pleasure to be able to tell this world leader in his geological field that the *Answers in Genesis*

ministries group would, stepping out in reliance on our supporters, fund his salary for such research work. (Dr. Silvestru has since emigrated to work full-time for Answers in Genesis in Canada).

References and notes

1. He was so named because he was a knight of the order of the dragon (*draco* in Latin, *drac* in ancient Romanian).

2. Dr. Silvestru told us, "According to our history, he constantly impaled thieves and pick-pockets. Therefore, foreign visitors were amazed to find out that a purse full of gold left in the middle of the road would stay there for days, as nobody dared risk a 'high rise.' "

3. *Karst* is a term which initially referred to barren regions of mostly limestone and dolomite, noted for spectacular and distinctive land forms, and with substantial underground drainage features — caves, underground rivers, etc. It has come to refer more to the entire geosystem, above and below ground — see also note 5.

4. This is the closest equivalent in western terms — it included a 60-page dissertation.

5. This discipline approaches karst as a geosystem. Dr. Silvestru says, "Karstology therefore deals with all features (above and below ground, physical and biological) related to limestones, including, for example, the sources of most of the rivers reaching the limestones."

6. There is some confusion between the Anglo-Saxon and Latin understanding of "karst," which Romanian and French pioneers in this work, principally Dr. Silvestru, are attempting to clarify with more rigorous geological terminology.

7. *Pneumatolysis*: The alteration of rock or crystallization of minerals by gaseous emanations from the late stages of a solidifying magma.

8. By Michael Oard and Dr. Larry Vardiman.

9. Some of these are being published with financial help from the *Answers in Genesis* ministries group.

10. F.G. Banting and C.H. Best, in 1921.

Photo by D. Seliscan

Awesome Mind

Gary Bates

talks to one of

Christianity's

foremost

defenders,

Jonathan Sarfati

Dr. Jonathan Sarfati obtained a B.Sc. (Hons.) in chemistry with two physics papers submitted (nuclear and condensed matter physics). His Ph.D. in chemistry was awarded for a thesis entitled "A Spectroscopic Study of Some Chalcogenide Ring and Cage Molecules." He has co-authored papers in mainstream scientific journals on high-temperature superconductors and selenium-containing ring- and cage-shaped molecules.

Very few people interested in creation/evolution issues will not have heard of Jonathan Sarfati. His books have become best sellers — standard fare for Christians wishing to engage those who hold to evolutionary/long-age ideas. One of the reasons they have become such a powerful tool for Christianity is the amazing flow of his clear, crisp trademark logic,[1] which has "skewered" and silenced many an evolutionary detractor.

Christianity makes sense

Interestingly, it was logical reasoning, not an emotional need or life crisis, that led Jonathan to become a Christian. While studying at Victoria University of Wellington, New Zealand, some Christians befriended him. This caused him to investigate the claims of Christianity, which he found logical and entirely defensible. This ultimately led to his conversion at age 20. However, he still had much to learn in the field of *apologetics*, or logically defending the faith. He and a group of like-minded Christians, seeing the need for Christians to be prepared to give reasons for their faith (1 Peter 3:15), co-founded the Wellington Christian Apologetics Society <www.christian-apologetics.org>.

Early in his Christian walk, he experienced many "Christian compromisers" (as he calls them) who said the creation- versus-evolution debate was a side issue. Logically, Jonathan realized that

"When Christians start on the right foundations and apply the correct chronological timeframes to God's Word, they will be less prone to accepting faulty man-made interpretations. Many theologians and other believers take the ever-changing views of secular science and try to make the Bible fit those ideas."

if the Genesis account of the entrance of sin and death into God's perfect world was not real history, then it eradicated the very reason why Christ (the God-man) had to come to earth to save mankind from the penalty their sin justly demanded.

"Sarfati" means "Frenchman" in Hebrew. Despite having no religious upbringing, Jonathan was driven to investigate his Jewish roots after his conversion. As a Messianic Jew, he has also passionately imbibed knowledge about church history and theological issues.[2] This has helped make him one of the world's most powerful defenders of the authority of the Bible.

People who meet Jonathan are left with no doubt that he has little time for those whom he feels distort, and therefore damage, the integrity of the Word of God. This led him to approach Dr. Carl Wieland (joint CEO of AIG International) to work for the ministry. Jonathan remarks, "I saw AiG at the cutting edge of this war, and I wanted to be part of the battle."

Carl recalls that time, "It always gets my attention when Ph.D. scientists offer their services to the ministry, considering they could often earn a substantial income in their specialist fields. But normally I would be more cautious; for example, giving time for someone to immerse themselves even more fully in cutting-edge creation literature. However, after a very brief interaction with Jonathan, I was immensely keen to hire him. Here was someone the Lord had blessed with a brilliant mind like a steel trap, and with a burning passion for what we were doing. I had no doubt that he would quickly do what he did, which was to devour everything worthwhile ever written on creation, and surge ahead of the pack."

Carl shared a typical example of Jonathan's amazing abilities. Reviewing a layman's article recently submitted by an expert on relativity, Jonathan circled a number which "had to be wrong." To explain why, he had attached photocopied pages, containing one of the classic equations of relativity from the book *Einstein's Universe*. Half-apologetically, Jonathan murmured, "This equation stuck in my mind since reading the book." Not recognizing the title from AiG's research library, Carl asked where he had obtained it.

"It was given to me on my birthday," was the reply. Which one? His fifteenth. His c. 25-year recall of an equation *outside* his specialist field instantly told him the article's number was a "typo"!

But prick him and he does bleed. In fact, one of the things that genuinely upsets him is seeing Christians "twisting" Scripture. It would be fair to say that he has more intellectual respect for an "out and out" atheist than for someone who reinterprets God's Word away from its intended meaning.

I now regard "Jono" (as he has become affectionately known) as a friend as well as a colleague. But before I joined AiG full-time, my own introduction to him was via email contact and from reading his *Refuting Evolution*. I can remember almost being in a state of disbelief at the man's recall of information and his "take-no-prisoners" style of writing. He has mellowed somewhat, and his approach overall is not without a measure of grace. This was demonstrated recently when he answered some criticisms from a homosexual man in the feedback section of the AiG website,[3] for which he received many positives for his sensitivity.

Going "Jono" on evolution

Many detractors still quote the old canard, "No real scientist believes in creation." But Jonathan definitely fits the description of a real scientist, and a brilliant one at that. He has published in a number of secular journals, including co-authoring a paper in the major journal *Nature* when only 21 years old.

His first book for AiG quickly became a landmark publication (about 350,000 copies and still growing). *Refuting Evolution* was a response to the aggressive action of the National Academy of Sciences in America. Convinced that creation was gaining a foothold, they produced a handbook of the "latest and greatest" evidences for evolution. Called *Teaching About Evolution and the Nature of Science*, it was distributed free to over 100,000 U.S. science teachers.

Jonathan's response systematically demolished their arguments. He believes that it is a Christian's duty to destroy any fallacies that have the potential to lead people astray. One of his favorite Bible passages is 2 Corinthians 10:5: "We demolish arguments and every pretension that sets itself up against the knowledge of God, and we take captive every thought to make it obedient to Christ."

Some years ago, while in America, Jonathan was asked to produce a response to the multi-million-dollar PBS/Nova television series, "Evolution." This was backed by prominent evolutionary humanists who invested millions, and launched with much hype and fanfare. Rabidly anti-creationist groups like the National Center for Science Education even had the audacity to entice Christians to accept the ideas presented in the programs by producing a free "church study guide." It was clear they were on the attack, their weapons aimed right at the very foundations of the Christian faith. So after each evening broadcast, Jonathan worked into the early morning hours producing a comprehensive critique, which appeared on the AiG website later that morning. His collection of responses to each episode of the series (www.AnswersInGenesis.org/pbs)

eventually formed a major part of AiG's famous *Creation* CD-Rom. Tens of thousands have been distributed all over the globe.

But wait, there's more

The value of having a formidable talent who can quickly provide such solid answers — especially to Christians who feel intimidated by a barrage of the so-called "facts" of evolution — cannot be overestimated. When the next evolutionary assault came, the Lord again turned what was meant for evil into good. The world famous journal *Scientific American* (SciAm) produced what they believed would be a "knockout blow" to the creationist cause. Their editor, John Rennie, wrote a multi-page lead article entitled "15 Answers to Creationist Nonsense." It was poorly researched and full of fallacious arguments. Once again, Jonathan worked furiously to produce a brilliant response which appeared on the AiG website within a few days (see <www. AnswersInGenesis.org/sciam>).

The gossip on the skeptics' own websites suggested that SciAm had suffered a financial downturn as a result of their "mistake." SciAm even made lame noises about legal action. Jono's SciAm response went on to form the basis of his second book, *Refuting Evolution 2*, which has also become a best seller and powerful witnessing tool.

Audiences in awe

One of Jonathan's other passions is chess, and like most things that he undertakes, he sets a standard which few in the world can match. A former New Zealand chess champion, he represented New Zealand in three Chess Olympiads, and he has drawn a tournament game with former world champion Boris Spassky. The International Chess Federation (F.I.D.E.) awarded him the title of F.I.D.E. Master (FM) in 1988.

At many AiG conferences and camps, he has become famous for his "chess challenges" against multiple players simultaneously — while blindfolded, with his "seeing" opponents'

Jonathan playing chess blindfolded against multiple players at AiG conference.

moves called out to him. At a recent AiG event in Sydney, Australia, he achieved a "personal best" by playing 12 opponents at once in this way.[4] A visiting creationist, a full professor at a leading UK university, was "text messaging" his wife, saying, "This is astounding — world-class — the world's media should be here!"

A day later, another AiG scientist told Jonathan what one of the competitors (no slouch at chess) had said after the game. The competitor had said he felt helpless against "what was obviously a formidable mind — but with a keenly developed sense of humor." The scientist mentioned (mistakenly) that it was the competitor on board number "x." In a flash, Jonathan replied, "No, it must have been the game one further to the left." With only this sketchy abstract opinion about his supposed strategy, he had correctly identified which game it was!

Jono has done this sort of thing many times over the years, so far undefeated. It is truly astonishing to watch — every position and move retained in his head over grueling hours, responding within seconds to his opponents' every move. For most "mere mortals" like me, this kind of "brain power" is an almost unimaginable gift.

Restoring the foundations

Jonathan's mission is to help restore the church to its biblical roots. He says, "When Christians start on the right foundations and apply the correct chronological time frames to God's Word, they will be less prone to accepting faulty man-made interpretations. Many theologians and other believers take the ever-changing views of secular science and try to make the Bible fit those ideas." He adds, "This is taking a low view of Scripture. They are placing the words of men above the very words of God. If we marry the Bible to today's science, then the Bible will be widowed tomorrow" (Ps. 18:30; 2 Sam. 22:31).

It is this "high view" of Scripture that motivated Jonathan's latest project, the book called *Refuting Compromise*. He left no stone unturned in dissecting what he says is the "distorted eisegesis" (reading things into the text) of Dr. Hugh Ross and his Reasons to Believe ministry. When I asked Jonathan why it was necessary to critique the beliefs of another Christian organization, he said, "AiG has never accused Dr. Ross of not being a Christian, and has explicitly stated that a young-earth belief is *not* a necessity for salvation. However, his ministry very much tries to reconcile the incorrect interpretations of many evolutionary scientists with the Bible, and it is leading many Christians astray from the original meaning of the Scriptures. For example, Ross believes in the big bang and its time frame of billions of years, so he 'reinterprets' Genesis 1 to mean that each 'day' is a long, in-determinate period of time; that there were soul-less human-like creatures before Adam, Noah's flood was local, and much more."

Jonathan adds, "Such views completely undermine the gospel of Christ, as my book explains. How could God declare his creation as 'very good' if there was death and disease before Adam, especially when Paul calls death 'the last enemy' [1 Cor. 15:26]? Sadly, Dr. Ross tries to spiritualize 'death,' as he does many other straightforward teachings in the Bible.

"This is serious, because Paul contrasts the death that Adam brought with the resurrection from the dead that the Last Adam (Christ) introduced, which all orthodox Christians must believe was bodily or physical [1 Cor. 15:21–22, 45]. Ross's 'spiritualization' of such basic tenets causes the Bible to become increasingly meaningless and irrelevant to those who are dying outside of Christ.

"What is even more worrying is that Ross's ideas have influenced some Christian leaders and Bible colleges. *I believe such views are, in fact, one of the greatest dangers to Christianity.*"

The just-released *Refuting Compromise* is an outstanding work, and Jonathan's best to date. I asked him what he wanted to achieve with it. In a softening tone he said, "My hope is that people will see this as a positive affirmation of the Bible's history and time scale, and see that the Bible really is revelation from God our Creator." Amen to that, Jono!

A privilege to know

For those of us who work with Jonathan every day, it would be easy to take his abilities for granted. Personally, I'm in awe of Jonathan's abilities, though more in awe of the One who made him. I'm also thankful that our great God led him to work for AiG. His example encourages us all to ". . . in your hearts set apart Christ as Lord. Always be prepared to give an answer to everyone who asks you to give the reason for the hope that you have. But do this with gentleness and respect" (1 Pet. 3:15). In short, along with tens of thousands around the globe, I'm really glad that Jono is on our side — and the Lord's.

References and notes

1. See Jonathan's outstanding *TJ* article, "Loving God With All Your Mind: Logic and Creation," TJ 12(2):142–151, 1998; <www.answersingenesis.org/logic>.

2. See *Jesus in Genesis: The Messianic Prophecies,* DVD. Recorded at AiG-Australia's SuperCamp, Sydney, 2004. Available from Answers in Genesis.

3. See <www.answersingenesis.org/gay-response>.

4. His previous best was winning 11/11 at the Kapiti Chess Club in New Zealand; E. Roberts, New Zealand Chess 29(3):23, June 2003.

The laws of physical science and the origin of life

Jonathan's training in chemistry enables him to see through the flaws in chemical evolution (aka abiogenesis), the materialistic theory that life came from non-living chemicals (see <www.answersingenesis.org/origin>). In his university days, the head of organic chemistry gave three lectures defending chemical evolution, then invited Jonathan to give one lecture on "loopholes" in these models. After the lecture, the professor admitted to the class, "If a vote were taken, I would surely come out worse. Jonathan has raised many hurdles — major hurdles."

But it wasn't actually so difficult — many of them came from the professor's own lucid teachings in the real chemistry lectures! This just shows how creationists and evolutionists have the same facts, but interpret them differently.

For example, many of life's chemicals come in two forms, "left-handed" and "right-handed." Life requires polymers with all building blocks having the same "handedness" (homochirality) — proteins have only "left-handed" amino acids, while DNA and RNA have only "right-handed" sugars. But ordinary undirected chemistry, as in the hypothetical primordial soup, would produce an equal mixture of left- and right-handed molecules, called a racemate. But even a slight impurity of the wrong-handed molecule can prevent

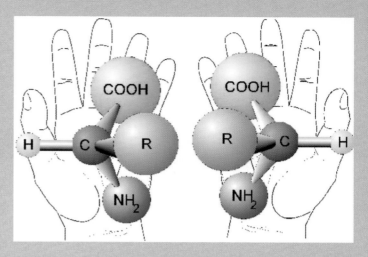

the required long molecules from forming.

Also, the supposed "building blocks" don't combine to form the long molecules (polymers) required for life. Jonathan says, "Rather, the reverse happens, especially in water! (That is, the long molecules disintegrate back into building blocks.) Another huge problem, remembered from long hours in the lab, is the way the molecules don't always combine in the right way. Food chemists know, for example, how sugars and amino acids will react self-destructively. This means tedious steps of purification, adding or removing special 'protecting groups' and controlling the sequence carefully. But there were no organic chemists to do that with the alleged primordial soup!"

Jonathan's favorite scientific evidences for a designer

Jonathan has written a number of articles for *Creation* and *TJ* on the amazing designs in creation (also posted at <www.AnswersInGenesis.org/design>). Some of his favorites are those that are giving human designers great ideas, a field called biomimetics. Some examples are the geometric eyes of lobsters inspiring X-ray telescope design, the dragonfly's pursuit system that can make it appear stationary, spider silk giving lessons to chemists preparing ultra-strong materials, a sponge's spicules that are almost unbreakable optical fibers, geckos' sticky feet inspiring powerful and self-cleaning adhesives, the world's tiniest motors (inside a cell), and the sense of smell that likely works on the principles of his own specialist area, vibrational spectroscopy.

Meet a leading scientist whose work has included research on the material used in space-age applications and the bulletproof vest — and who believes the Bible from cover to cover.

Don Batten and Jonathan Sarfati talk to research chemist Patrick Young

Dr. Patrick H. Young, B.S., Ph.D., is a technical service manager at the DuPont Laboratories in Ohio. He is the holder of patents related to Kevlar (which is used in bullet-resistant vests, for example) and Mylar (the magnetic tape in video cassette recorders), with two other patents pending. His outstanding achievements have earned him awards and recognition, including being voted one of the outstanding young men of America in 1989, and one of the outstanding young men of science in 1993.

In today's violence-ridden times, television footage of police wearing bulletproof (bullet-resistant is perhaps the more proper, but less used term) vests is familiar to many. Perhaps not everyone, though, knows that the bullet-proof material used in these vests is a synthetic fiber called Kevlar, which is 10 percent stronger than steel by weight. We recently spoke to a senior research scientist at DuPont, the makers of Kevlar. Dr. Patrick Young, though not the actual inventor of Kevlar (that was a Dr. Stephanie Kwolek), holds patents related to the processes of its manufacture.

He told us more about this fascinating material. "Its strength lies in its chemical structure. It is spun as a liquid crystal, forming a very rigid rod polymer, and when it's oriented it's very stiff.

Bullet Proofing
BELIEF

That particular characteristic, plus the fact that it really has no melting point (in fact, it decomposes before it melts), gives it flame-retardant properties. It's used a lot in airplanes for that reason, also in automobile brake and clutch pads. There are many different applications for Kevlar, besides the one everyone thinks about— bulletproof vests."

Dr. Young has extensively researched Kevlar's bullet-proof characteristics. "It is an interesting mechanism. Its chemical structure enables it to stop a bullet by flattening out and thus absorbing the impact energy."

As pleased as Dr. Young was to tell us of his work with bullet-resistant vests, it wasn't long before the conversation turned to something he considers much more important — namely, having a bullet-resistant faith. This leading researcher speaks passionately of his concerns for the many people who do not understand the fundamental importance to Christianity of the Genesis creation account. "I run into many professing Christians who believe, for example, that 'God used evolution to create.' I'm flabbergasted that they don't understand that if you throw away Adam, the Fall, and the original sin, then you throw away Jesus Christ and His reason for coming, and the whole thing falls like a house of cards."

Patrick Young says, "I was taught evolution in high school, and though I was raised in a Christian environment, nobody was standing up and opposing it, so it was kind of just migrating into my mind and staying there."

He says he probably dealt with this by "trying not to think about it . . . there were many other things on my mind, going through school, studying chemistry. My training in Christianity was more of a 'New Testament only' thing, with emphasis mostly on Christian living. Thankfully, in the last 10–15 years, God

> *"One often hears the myth repeated that without evolution, science and technology would collapse. But not only did science and technology flower on a foundation of biblical creation, scientists like Dr. Young, whose research has impacted on cutting-edge technology, testify that evolution has contributed nothing to their science."*

has given me a hunger to go back into the Old Testament . . . and I now know that Genesis is crucial to understanding the gospel."

In his daily work, Patrick sees the hand of the Creator. He says, "The whole world of chemistry is a well-behaved world. If you understand the principles of it, you can do a great deal to control it. To me, that's evidence of design and a designer right there! If all that came about by chance (as evolutionists claim), I do not believe that the world of chemistry would be as well-behaved as it is."

Dr. Young's comments are consistent with the thinking of the successful pioneer scientists, who believed that God is a God of order. Therefore, especially since we are made in God's image, we should be able to understand the world to a substantial extent. (In fact, contrary to the common claims in the media and educational circles, this Christian/creationist view provided the very foundation of modern science.) Dr. Young affirms that his success in research chemistry is founded on this basic philosophy. And he is quick to acknowledge that for all man's ingenuity and breakthroughs in developing high performance man-made fibers, they yet fall short of the God-designed "natural" fibers such as spider silk. (See box on page 105.)

We are often told that "no real scientist" disbelieves in evolution. So we asked this leading chemist, a "real scientist" by any definition, what he thought of the evolutionary idea of life evolving from lifeless chemicals in some primordial soup. He said, "I've read a great deal on that; it's clearly a gross oversimplification to state that if some simulated lightning is put into a beaker and creates some amino

Dr. Patrick Young

acids, you are on the way to making life. One needs to realize that to go further from this point your experiment would need to have developed only certain specific types of amino acids, either the dextrorotatory ('right-handed') or the levorotatory ('left-handed') type — and guess what?! That doesn't happen — nobody has been able to do that, and so the 'primordial soup' belief system has absolutely no scientific evidence to support it."[1]

Dr. Young says, "Probably 90–95 percent of the people who tell me they believe in evolution, when I ask them to tell me why, cannot do so. They can't explain it in a scientific manner, but when they come across somebody who can explain creation in a scientifically valid manner, they kind of just turn around and walk away."

So why don't more scientists, with all their education, recognize the fact of the Creator?

Dr. Young is forthright: "Most of the scientists I come across, I believe that they wake up in the morning, look in the mirror and see their god. I think there is a level of arrogance in the scientific community and that is probably the reason why they don't have the belief system needed for God — because they would first have to crucify that arrogance.

"The key to a person's thinking stretches back to the foundations of their education," says Dr. Young. He is critical of the U.S. public education system's handling of the creation/evolution debate, which, he says, "attempts to brainwash children to go in a certain direction," that is, undermining the very foundations of Christianity.

Little wonder, says Dr. Young, that so many Christians today are ineffective when it comes to sharing their faith. "The frozen chosen" he calls them, sadly — paralyzed through a lack of understanding of the foundational truths of the Gospel.

To reinforce his point, Dr. Young draws an analogy between being effective as a chemist and being effective as a Christian. "In chemistry, you need to first grasp the basic foundational principles. As a chemist, if I have that basic foundation of chemistry, then when I start actually doing the research, it's that foundation that makes things so much easier, so I can be much more creative. So, too, with Christianity; to be effective one must have a sound understanding of the foundations — and that means understanding creation and Fall and their relevance to the gospel.

"Sadly," says Dr. Young, "teaching on Genesis is generally very poor." But he is greatly heartened to see that Christians are beginning to wake up to the importance of this issue.

He says, "I remember listening to Ken Ham in a seminar a few weeks ago; he did a phenomenal job on teaching a proper understanding of Genesis, and it was just amazing to see the number of people whose eyes were as big as saucers when they walked out of there! They said, 'I really didn't know that!' — and they had been Christians for years."

As Dr. Young affirms from his own experience, the effect of a fuller understanding of Genesis and the gospel not only helps make one's own faith more "bulletproof," but equips Christians with the confidence to go out and share the good news with others, as the Lord commanded in Matthew 28:19–20.

He excitedly explains: "As far as I am concerned now, my basic role in life is to be someone who follows God and His purposes, and God has placed me in a unique position in my work. I travel a great deal, interact with many people, and am able to speak about certain things, so I find openings to talk about some things that may plant 'gospel seeds.'

"I've always told my wife that I have an interesting ministry flying in a passenger aircraft at high altitude because I've got a captive audience — they can't go anywhere."

At the end of our talk, Dr. Young was warmly and spontaneously appreciative of the *Answers in Genesis* ministry. He said, "I believe it is something that needs to keep on happening. I'll continue to cover the AiG ministry in prayer because I believe you are at the front line of those who are proclaiming the Word of God, so the devil will definitely keep on attacking your marvellous work."

We felt privileged to have spoken to a strong Christian, passionate about sharing his faith, who also happens to be one of the leading industrial research scientists in the world.

References and notes

1. Questions and Answers, Origin of life, <www.answersingenesis.org/home/area/faq/origin.asp>.

While Kevlar is the "gold medalist"[1] of man-made fibers because of its bullet-stopping abilities, it's overshadowed in many ways by the humble spider web. "Spider silk is stronger and more elastic than Kevlar, and Kevlar is the strongest man-made fiber," according to Danish spider expert Fritz Vollrath.[2] Dragline silk, the main support for its web, is a hundred times stronger than steel — a cable of this silk a little thicker than a garden hose could support the weight of two full Boeing 737 aircraft.[3] It can also stretch to 40 percent of its length,[4] while the flagelliform silk in web spirals can stretch to over 200 percent.[5]

The manufacture of Kevlar requires harsh conditions, including the boiling of sulfuric acid and the leaving behind of dangerous chemicals that are expensive to dispose of.[6] But spiders need only ordinary temperatures, and they use a much milder acid bath, which is produced by special ducts.[7]

Spiders can make silk at different speeds — up to ten times faster when dropping to escape a predator — unlike most industrial chemical processes that would make "gunk" if the speed was varied by that much. Spider silk is even environmentally friendly — spiders eat their own webs when they no longer need them.[8]

Spider silk owes its amazing strength and elasticity to its "complexity that makes synthetic fibers seem crude."[9] Man-made fibers are usually just simple strands of material, but a silk fiber has a core surrounded by concentric layers of nanofibrils (tiny threads). Some layers contain nanofibrils aligned parallel to the axis, while other layers contain nanofibrils coiling like a spiral staircase. The coiled ones allow the silk to be stretched, because they simply straighten up rather than break.

The nanofibrils themselves are very complicated, containing tiny protein crystals in an amorphous (shapeless) matrix of tangled protein chains. These nanocrystals contain electrical charges that stop the chains from slipping, so providing strength, while the amorphous material is rubbery and allows the fiber to stretch.

Some researchers have tried to make silk by forcing a solution of silk proteins, called spidroin, through tiny holes, but the fibers are less than half as strong as those produced by the spider. It seems that the spider produces the high complexity required by making the spidroin go through a liquid crystal phase, where rod-shaped molecules align parallel (Kevlar manufacture also uses a liquid crystal phase). Christopher Viney, of Heriot–Watt University in Edinburgh, believes that this enables them to flow more easily, thus saving energy.[10] The liquid state also aligns the protein molecules so they can form the nanocrystals and coiled nanofibrils. This seems to occur in the spider's long s-duct, where water is both squeezed and pumped out. This brings hydrophobic (water-repelling) parts of the proteins to the outside and forms the nanocrystals and enables the fibers to form.

Spiders normally now use their webs for trapping insects and other prey. But some baby spiders catch pollen for food,[11] providing a possible clue to a pre-Fall function for the spider web.[12]

References and notes

1. D. Fox, "The Spinners," New Scientist 162(2183):38–41, April 24, 1999. See p. 1 for the quote on which our title here is based.

2. "How Spiders Make Their Silk, Discover 19(10):34, October 1998.

3. E. Stokstad, "Spider Genes Reveal Flexible Design," Science 270(5457):1378, February 25, 2000.

4. Fox, "The Spinners."

5. Stokstad, "Spider Genes Reveal Flexible Design."

6. Fox, "The Spinners."

7. "How Spiders Make Their Silk."

8. Ibid.

9. Fox, "The Spinners."

10. Ibid.

11. Nature Australia 26(7):5, Summer 1999–2000.

12. "Pollen-eating Spiders," Creation 22(3):5, 2000.

EPILOGUE

Our introduction explained why it is important to "explode the myth" that believing God's Word about history is incompatible with high academic and scientific prowess and achievement.

But whether we were to parade tens of thousands of Bible-believing scientists in front of you, or whether it turned out that not a single scientist believed the Bible, it would not make the slightest difference to the truth. Because, as will hopefully now be clear, this is ultimately not an intellectual issue. The Bible says that people are naturally inclined away from God. Romans Chapter 1 talks of those who "did not like to retain God in their knowledge." It says of these: "Professing themselves to be wise, they became fools" and they "changed the truth of God into a lie, and worshipped and served the creature [the created thing — nature, other people, the idols of any age] more than the Creator, who is blessed for ever" (Romans 1:22-25).

The real reason for rejecting Genesis is because it gives an "excuse" for rejecting the rest of the Bible, which all points to our sinfulness and need for a Savior.

Because of our sinful nature, we are deserving of God's wrath in eternity, unless we cast ourselves unconditionally upon His mercy, through the sacrificial death and resurrection of Jesus Christ, the "last Adam," God the Son, the Creator made flesh. The good news is that this same Lord Jesus says (John 5:24): "I tell you the truth, whoever hears my word and believes him who sent me has eternal life and will not be condemned; he has crossed over from death to life."

As individuals, we can all get involved in spreading what we call the creation/gospel message, so needed in today's world. Namely that the history recorded in Genesis is not only crucial to the gospel, but is true, and along with it the rest of the Bible.

– Carl Wieland

ABOUT THE AUTHORS

DON BATTEN, B.Sc.Agr.(Hons.), Ph.D.

Dr. Batten is a consultant plant physiologist and research scientist who works full-time for Answers in Genesis in Brisbane, Australia.

CARL WIELAND, M.B., B.S.

Dr. Wieland is CEO of Answers in Genesis in Brisbane, Australia, and CEO of Answers in Genesis International. He was founding editor of *Creation* magazine.

GARY BATES

Gary heads the Ministry Development Department of Answers in Genesis in Brisbane, Australia. He was previously a business proprietor and volunteer state coordinator/speaker for Answers in Genesis in Western Australia.

MARK LOOY, M.A.

Mark is a co-founder of Answers in Genesis-USA in Florence, Kentucky, where he is vice-president of ministry relations.

JONATHAN SARFATI, B.Sc.(Hons), Ph.D., F.M.

Dr. Sarfati's Ph.D. in physical chemistry is from Victoria University, Wellington, New Zealand. He is the author of the best-selling *Refuting Evolution*. A former New Zealand chess champion, he works full-time for Answers in Genesis in Australia.

CHRIS FIELD

Chris is a pastor based in Melbourne, Australia who has produced many Christian programs for community television. He is a keen supporter of Answers in Genesis.

Additional Photo Credits

O LORD, our Lord, how majestic is your name in all the earth!

You have set your glory above the heavens. From the lips of children and infants you have ordained praise because of your enemies, to silence the foe and the avenger.

When I consider your heavens, the work of your fingers, the moon and the stars, which you have set in place, what is man that you are mindful of him, the son of man that you care for him? You made him a little lower than the heavenly beings and crowned him with glory and honour. You made him ruler over the works of your hands; you put everything under his feet: all flocks and herds, and the beasts of the field, the birds of the air, and the fish of the sea, all that swim the paths of the seas.

O LORD, our Lord, how majestic is your name in all the earth!

– Psalm 8